KAY ARTHUR

How to Study Your Bible

HARVEST HOUSE PUBLISHERS
EUGENE, OREGON 97402

Cover by Koechel Peterson & Associates, Inc., Minneapolis, Minnesota

HOW TO STUDY YOUR BIBLE

Copyright © 1994 by Precept Ministries
Published by Harvest House Publishers
Eugene, Oregon 97402
www.harvesthousepublishers.com

Library of Congress Cataloging-in-Publication Data
Arthur, Kay, 1933–
    [How to study your Bible precept upon precept]
    How to study your Bible / Kay Arthur.
        p.   cm.
      Originally published: How to study your Bible precept upon precept. Old Tappan, NJ: F.H. Revell, c1985.
    ISBN 0-7369-0544-8
    1. Bible—Study and teaching.   I. Title.
    BS600.2.A77   1994
    220'.07—dc20
                                           93-31606
                                              CIP

Printed in the United States of America

05 06 07 08 09 10 11 12 13 / ML / 19 18 17 16 15 14 13 12 11

Contents

PART FIVE
Practical Helps—Tools for Further Study

Acknowledgments

Although this book bears my name, it is a team effort. My original work, begun approximately 20 years ago, has been edited, supplemented, polished, and refined by Precept Ministries' Training Team, headed up by Betsy Bird, our Developer of Training and Pete DeLacy, our Director of Training. This dedicated team of men and women, along with our Precept Trainers worldwide, bring to this book years of experience. Together they have trained thousands of people from all walks of life to study the Bible using the Precept Upon Precept method of inductive study. In fact our Precept Upon Precept Inductive Study Courses are now in 15 languages with more in process.

People who never graduated from high school as well as seminary graduates have said over and over that the **Precept Training Workshops** and/or the doing of a **Precept Course** taught them more than they had ever experienced before, or in many cases, more than they thought they could ever learn.

Thus this book is a combined effort of men and women from across this nation, Canada, and many parts of the world who have the same passion—to establish God's people in God's Word as that which produces reverence for Him (Psalm 119:38). That group of people also includes every one of Precept Ministries' homebase staff of about 120 men and women, who each in their faithfulness to their task have contributed in their own valuable way.

And for that reason this book is dedicated...

- ∾ to Precept's Training Team at the home base,

- ∾ to our Precept Trainers who live across this nation and in various parts of the world and who travel wherever they're sent (even to Siberia),

- ∾ to every faithful Precept Leader here and around the world who spends hours each week studying God's Word so that others might know Him, and,

~ to our beloved staff who "stand by the stuff" day in and day out working unitedly for the glory of One and One alone, our head, the Lord Jesus Christ.

We all do this joyfully, grateful to God for His calling, for we know and believe that "the people who know their God will be strong and do exploits" for Him (Daniel 11:32b)—and that is what our world desperately needs more than anything else.

To each of you, Beloved, I say:

May the Lord reward your work,
and your wages be full from the Lord, the God of Israel,
under whose wings you have come to seek refuge.
RUTH 2:12

If You Want to Know God's Word...

～～～～～

Beloved,

Do you realize that you are about to learn a method of Bible study that could be your launching pad to a life of new vision and renewed hope? Throughout the ages, God has raised up men and women, ordinary people like you and me, and used them to accomplish great works for His kingdom. As you begin, my prayer for you is that through the study of His Word, God will let you see the vital significance of your life. I pray that you will persevere and not lose heart. Greatness is never achieved nor dreams realized apart from great discipline.

In 1969, my husband, Jack, and I returned from the mission field because of an illness I had. He became the station manager for a Christian radio station. I was asked to teach a Bible study with 250 women every week in Atlanta, Georgia. The hunger these women had to know God's Word and apply it in a deeply personal way to their everyday lives touched me.

The first draft of *How to Study Your Bible* was four pages long, printed on a mimeograph machine. My heart's cry to God during those years was "Lord, when you call me to leave Atlanta and these 250 people, will they be able to feed themselves?"

Out of that experience, Precept Upon Precept Inductive Bible Courses were born, and the class in Atlanta grew from 250 to 1700. Over the past 20 years, this nondenominational Bible study ministry has helped hundreds of thousands of men and women in the United States and over 85 countries learn to study the Bible inductively, "precept upon precept," through classes and seminars.

While learning in a group setting is extremely valuable to most people, there are others who want to learn to study the Bible on their own. That is the purpose of this book.

If you long to know God, if you yearn for a deep and abiding relationship with Jesus Christ, if you want to live the Christian life faithfully and know what God requires of you, you must do more than

7

merely read the Bible and study what someone else has said about it. You must interact with God's Word personally, absorbing its message and letting God engrave His truth on your heart and mind and life. That is the very heart of inductive study: seeing truth for yourself, discerning what it means, and applying that truth to your life.

The accuser of the brethren, the devil, will seek to discourage you on every hand (John 8:44; Revelation 12:10), especially if you have tried studying the Bible before and failed. He will attempt to persuade you that it is just too hard for you, that you will never get it, that it is useless to try.

How I wish I could talk with you face-to-face so I could encourage you, challenge you, and support you—so that you can discipline yourself for the goal of godliness. These are critical times, and I know that only those "who know their God will be strong and do exploits for Him" (Daniel 11:32b KJV). What an hour for the church to hold forth the Word of life in the midst of a crooked and perverse generation.

May God grant you a vision of what He can do in your life through inductive Bible study, and may you persevere until that vision becomes reality. God bless you. May He use you far beyond your wildest dreams!

—*Kay Arthur*

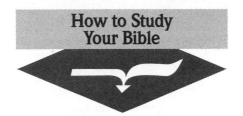

THE JOY AND VALUE OF INDUCTIVE STUDY

*T*he Bible was written so that anyone who wants to know who God is and how they are to live in a way that pleases Him can read it and find out.

God wants to bring us into intimacy with Himself. He wants to be a Father to us. In order to have that relationship, however, God has to talk to us. He wants to explain to us who He is and how we can be brought into a close, wonderful relationship with Him. He also wants us to understand the blessings of a life of obedience to His Word and the consequences of disobeying Him. And He wants us to know the truth about life and what is going to happen in the the future.

The Bible tells us everything we need to know about life. That my friend, is why you need to study it for yourself.

There are many ways to study the Bible, and there are many excellent study aids available to help you with specific books of the Bible. But the most important thing you need to remember is that to find out what the Bible says, you need to read it yourself in a way that will help you discover what it says, what it means, and how you are to apply it to your life. And the best way to do this is through the process called inductive study. Inductive study doesn't tell you what the Bible means or what you should believe. Instead, it teaches you a method of

9

studying God's Word that can be applied to any portion of Scripture at any time for the rest of your life.

The main requirement in learning to study the Bible inductively is the willingness to slow down and really look at what the Scripture is saying. That may not sound too difficult, but in times like ours it is probably the most difficult part of the entire process. And to be honest, my friend, don't you sometimes wonder if our busyness—even for God—isn't often what's keeping us from being what God wants us to be?

Inductive Bible study uses the Bible itself as the primary source of information about the Bible. In inductive study you personally explore the Scriptures apart from conclusions Bible scholars and other people have drawn from their study of the Word. Though their labors are valuable, research has shown time and time again that people learn more and remember better when they enter into the process of discovery for themselves. In inductive study, commentaries, books, tapes, and other information about the Bible are consulted only after you have made your own thorough examination of the Scripture. These, then, can serve as a sounding board for your own observations and conclusions.

Actually, you may already be familiar with some of the principles of inductive study. For example, if you have ever taken any biology courses, you have studied frogs, and you have probably done so through observation.

To thoroughly study the frog, you first go to a river or creek bank where frogs live. You watch their eggs hatch and the tadpoles emerge. You see their back and front legs develop and grow, until they look like frogs and leave the water. After observing how the frogs respond to their new life on land, you catch one and observe it more closely. Eventually you take it to the biology lab where you dissect it to see how it looks on the inside. Afterward, you read what other biologists have learned about frogs to see if your conclusions match.

Inductive study of the Bible involves the same process: You begin with the Bible, observe it in its environment, and then take it apart so that you understand it firsthand. Then, when you've seen or discovered all you can on your own, you compare your observations with those of godly men and women who have written about the Word down through the ages.

Now, it would be much easier to just sit down and read a book about frogs in the first place and forget about traipsing through the marsh, wouldn't it? But you would end up with only secondhand knowledge. You would know what others have said about frogs, which might be interesting and—you hope—true. But you never would have had a personal encounter with a frog.

Inductive Bible study draws you into personal interaction with the Scripture and thus with the God of the Scriptures so that your beliefs are based on a prayerful understanding and legitimate interpretation of Scripture—truth that transforms you when you live by it.

If you will study inductively, the benefits will be beyond anything you have ever hoped could happen in your own personal under-standing of the Word of God. As a result of incorporating the principles of inductive Bible study that we present in this book, you will

    ∾ be equipped to study God's Word on your own

    ∾ be independent of relying only on another's interpretation

    ∾ increase your knowledge of God and His ways

    ∾ be greatly strengthened in your personal faith

    ∾ recognize the authority of the inerrant Word of God in your daily walk

    ∾ become increasingly aware of all that it means to be in Christ.

Well, my friend, that is what this study guide is all about. It's a manual designed to help you know and understand the Bible—to study it so you can see for yourself what it says about God, what it says about you, and what it says about becoming part of God's forever family.

Beginning with the Basics

Inductive Bible study consists of three component parts, which we will look at separately, but which frequently overlap in practice. These three parts are observation, interpretation, and application.

OBSERVATION

Observation answers the question: *What does the passage say?* It is the foundation which must be laid if you want to accurately interpret and properly apply God's Word. Have you ever read a book, chapter, or verse of the Bible and five minutes later been unable to remember anything you have read? So often we read the Bible with our eyes but not with our mind. There are several reasons for this. Either

∾ we think God's Word will magically make an impression on us without any effort on our part, or

∾ we don't really believe we can understand what we've read, or

∾ we are waiting for the pastor to teach on this section of Scripture so we'll know what to believe.

Often, however, we forget what we have read simply because we don't know what to look for in the text. Therefore, in the first part of this book you are going to learn what to look for when you read your Bible.

Because observation is discovering what the passage is saying, it requires time and practice. You'll discover that the more you read and get to know a book of the Bible, the more its truths will become obvious to you. You'll be awed at the wealth of spiritual riches contained in even the shortest books of the Bible—and you will have discovered it yourself! You will know that you know!

INTERPRETATION

Interpretation answers the question: *What does the passage mean?* And the basis for accurate interpretation is always careful observation. Interpretation is the process of discovering what the passage means. As you carefully observe Scripture, the meaning will become apparent. However, if you rush into interpretation without laying the vital foundation of accurate observation, your understanding will be colored by your presuppositions—what *you* think, what *you* feel, or what *other people* have said, rather than what God's Word says.

Interpretation is not necessarily a separate step from observation, for often, as you carefully observe the text, at that very moment you begin to see what it means. Thus, interpretation flows out of observation.

However, interpretation can also involve separate actions or steps that go beyond merely observing the immediate text. One of these exercises is investigating cross-references. First and foremost, let Scripture interpret Scripture. You may also use other helps, such as word studies or the evaluation of resources such as commentaries and Bible dictionaries to check your conclusions or to supplement your understanding of the historical or cultural setting of the text.

What we are going to do is to give you principles of interpretation and offer special sections to guide you in handling different types of writing, including figures of speech, parables, and allegories. We'll also show you how to do word studies and how to use Bible study tools that will greatly enhance your learning. It's going to be exciting—and so enlightening!

APPLICATION
Discover How It Works!

Application answers the question: *How does the meaning of this passage apply to me?* Usually this is the first thing we want to know when we read the Bible, but proper application actually begins with belief which then results in being and doing. Once you know what a passage means, you are not only responsible for putting it into practice in your own life, but accountable if you don't! Ultimately, then, the goal of personal Bible study is a transformed life and a deep and abiding relationship with Jesus Christ.

Application is not a third step in the inductive process. Rather, application takes place as you are confronted with truth and decide to respond in obedience to that truth. The basis for application is 2 Timothy 3:16-17:

> All Scripture is inspired by God and profitable for teaching, for reproof, for correction, for training in righteousness; so that the man of God may be adequate, equipped for every good work.

When you know what God says, what He means, and how to put His truths into practice, you will be equipped for every circumstance of life. To be equipped for every good work of life—totally prepared to handle every situation in a way that honors God—is not only possible, it is God's will. And that's what you will learn how to do if you will

13

apply these study principles. Oh, the hundreds of stories we could tell you about what God has done because people disciplined themselves to know His Word in this way. It would thrill your heart! But right now stories aren't our purpose; getting you into the Word inductively is! Then, friend, you can tell your own story! We'd love to hear it!

When you know what God says, what He means, and how to put His truths into practice, you will be equipped for every circumstance of life.

How Observation, Interpretation, and Application Relate to Each Other

Accurate **interpretation** and correct **application** rest on the accuracy of your **observations.** Therefore, it is vital that you develop observation skills, even if at first they seem time-consuming or you feel less than adequate and even awkward doing them. Studying inductively is a learning process that does not happen overnight. It happens by doing—doing over and over again, until the doing becomes almost a habit, and a wonderful one at that.

As you go through the inductive process, you'll sometimes find observation, interpretation, and application happening simultaneously. God can give you insight at any point in your study, so be sensitive to His leading. When words or passages make an impression on you, stop for a moment and meditate on what God has shown you. Bring the plumb line of truth against what you believe and how you are living.

When you know what God says, what He means, and how to put His truths into practice, you will be equipped for every circumstance of life.

Through a diligent study of God's Word, under the guidance of His Spirit, you'll drop a strong anchor that will hold in the storms of life. You will know your God. And when you know your God, not only will you be strong, but you will do great exploits for Him (Daniel 11:32).

Part One

OBSERVATION

Discover What It Says!

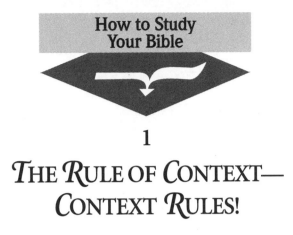

1

The Rule of Context— Context Rules!

*N*ow, let's sit down and begin. And where do you begin? You begin by observing the text as a whole. By the text we mean whatever portion of Scripture you want to study. We suggest you study the Bible book by book, because each book of the Bible is a complete message in and of itself that in turn relates in a special way to the whole Word of God. So choose your text—a book of the Bible—and then keep the following principles before you.

STEP ONE

Begin with Prayer

You are about to learn the most effective method of Bible study there is. Yet apart from the work of the Holy Spirit, that's all it will be—a method.

John 16:13-15 tells us that the One who guides us into all truth, the One who takes the things of God and reveals them to us, is the Holy Spirit, our resident Teacher. So ask God, by His Spirit, to lead you into all truth and to open your eyes that you may behold wondrous things out of His Word (see Psalm 119:18 KJV). Begin with prayer—and continue with an attitude of prayer.

STEP TWO

Identify the Context

Inductive study begins with a thorough evaluation of the context.

One of the most important principles of handling the Word properly and studying the Bible inductively is to interpret Scripture in the light of its context. Why? Because *context always rules in interpretation.*

The word *context* means "that which goes with the text." In general, then, context is the environment in which something dwells, the setting in which something exists or occurs. Remember the tadpole in the creek? Context is the creek!

In Bible study, context is the words, phrases, and sentences surrounding a particular word, phrase, or sentence. This context gives meaning to the particular word, phrase, or sentence and helps you understand what the author is saying. Context can also be expanded to paragraphs, chapters, books, and eventually the whole Bible. Because context rules in, or determines, the interpretation of the passage, it is important for you to know the context of any passage that you're studying.

To illustrate how context gives meaning to words, let's look at the word *trunk.* Suppose someone were to ask you, "What does the word *trunk* mean?" How would you respond? Well, if you were going to give a helpful as well as an accurate answer, you would first have to ask, "How is the word used?" because the word *trunk* can mean different things.

A trunk could mean the luggage compartment of a car, the flexible snout of an elephant, a large rigid piece of luggage used for transporting clothing and personal effects, the main stem of a tree, or shorts worn for swimming.

Therefore, the only way to know the intended meaning of the word *trunk* is to examine the context in which the word is used. The environment (the surrounding text) in which the word appears will show you which of these possible meanings is intended.

For instance, what would the word *trunk* mean in the following account from a trip to Africa?

> "I remember seeing this huge trunk appear before the window of our car. We had been informed to always line up our car in the same direction in which the elephant was going, in case he charged at our vehicle. As we saw this trunk swinging back and forth and the elephant's face coming closer, we knew it was time to leave!"

Since context is "that which surrounds or goes with the text," what information in this passage gives us a proper understanding of the word *trunk* as it is used here?

Well, we see that the word "elephant" appears twice, and the trunk is described as "huge" and "swinging back and forth." By examining the context, therefore, we discover the facts that surround the use of this word and can determine that in this particular passage the word *trunk* means "the flexible snout of an elephant."

In inductive study, context is determined or identified in the same way—by carefully observing what is repeated in the text and seeing how it all relates. If you observe what is said and pay attention to the repeated words, phrases, or ideas, you'll clearly see the context in any book, chapter, or passage that you're studying.

Context is determined or identified by thorough, careful observation of the text. Therefore...

STEP *THREE*

Observe the Obvious

When you observe the text, *begin by looking for things that are obvious*—in other words, *things that are easy to see.*

Facts about people, places, and events always capture our attention; therefore, people, places, and events are easy to see. Since these kinds of facts are often repeated, this also makes them easy to see.

If you keep your focus on the obvious, you will discover significant or repeated ideas; these will, in turn, show you the context of the book, chapter, passage, or verse you are studying.

For example, if you decide to put together a rectangular jigsaw puzzle, where do you start? Which pieces do you look for first? The four corners, of course! Why? Because they are obvious: There are only four of them, and they are easy to find because they have two straight sides.

Once you identify the four corners, what do you look for next? Naturally, you look for the next most obvious things: the straight edges. Once again, they're the easiest pieces to find because each has one straight side!

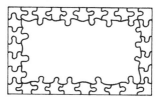

By the time you have connected the straight edges, you have an outline or framework within which to put the other pieces together. You have established the context for the puzzle by looking for the obvious.

In a similar fashion, looking for the obvious facts, details, or ideas establishes the framework in studying a book, chapter, or passage of the

Bible. So to put together a framework for the text, begin with the things that are obvious in that book.

As you observe the text and discover the context, however, you must always...

STEP FOUR

Deal with the Text Objectively

In other words, let the text speak for itself. Observing the text in order to establish context must be your primary objective, so let the text itself show you its repeated emphasis.

So often I fear our only reason for being in the Word is subjective—simply to get something for ourselves. To look for something that "ministers to our heart"—or to find a verse we can use to help someone or set someone straight.

How grievous this must be to God, who wants us to truly know Him and to be sanctified (set apart) by truth—and His Word is truth (John 17:17). Therefore, our primary goal—our driving passion—should be to know truth and then adjust our beliefs and our lives accordingly.

Now granted, certain portions of any book you are studying might minister to you more than other portions, but the truth and context never change. The message of the book itself will always be the same. It is truth—absolutes on which you can stake your life, your character, and your lifestyle.

So first, look at the Word objectively.

Yes, God's Word will minister to you personally. It will! It's a living Word. But to discover the context, you must first look at the text objectively to discover the repeated emphasis of the author. Then, when you personalize the Word, you'll know you are applying it correctly. And that's imperative.

Now as I say this, I must also caution you not to fail to look at Scripture subjectively as well. When you pause to reflect on what God is saying and how it applies to you, that is when God the Holy Spirit quickens His Word to your heart; that is when you know He has a message especially for you at a specific point in your life.

At the same time that you study the Bible inductively, read it devotionally. By devotionally I mean with a heart that wants to hear what God is saying to you. God speaks to us personally through His Word. Therefore as you read and as you study, don't fail to take time to listen to your God.

STEP FIVE

Read with a Purpose

Reading with a purpose is accomplished by asking questions of the text. You must interrogate the text as a detective would a witness.

To get the whole story—all the details—journalists are taught to ask the "5 W's and an H" (*who, what, when, where, why,* and *how*) in their reporting.

If you are going to read the Bible with purpose—to get all the details—**you must ask the 5 W's and an H**. Therefore, as you read, ask...

> **Who** wrote it? *Who* said it? *Who* are the major characters? *Who* are the people mentioned? To *whom* is the author speaking? About *whom* is he speaking?

> **What** are the main events? *What* are the major ideas? *What* are the major teachings? *What* are these people like? *What* does he talk about the most? *What* is his purpose in saying that?

> **When** was it written? *When* did this event take place? *When* will it happen? *When* did he say it? *When* did he do it?

> **Where** was this done? *Where* was this said? *Where* will it happen?

> **Why** was there a need for this to be written? *Why* was this mentioned? *Why* was so much or so little space devoted to this

particular event or teaching? *Why* was this reference mentioned? *Why* should they do such and such?

How is it done? *How* did it happen? *How* is this truth illustrated?

When you ask the 5 W's and an H of the text, and when you let the text provide the answers, you'll be amazed at what you learn. These questions are the building blocks of precise observation which, remember, lay a solid foundation for accurate interpretation.

However, *if you rush into interpretation without laying the vital foundation of observation, your understanding becomes colored by your own presuppositions*—what *you* think, what *you* feel, or what *other people* have said. And if you do this, you distort the Scriptures to your own destruction—something we are specifically warned against (2 Peter 3:16).

Many times Scripture is simply misinterpreted because the context isn't carefully observed. Accurate answers from the text to the 5 W's and an H kinds of questions will help assure correct interpretation.

Let me illustrate this by simply using one verse:

"After these things Jesus was walking in Galilee; for He was unwilling to walk in Judea because the Jews were seeking to kill Him" (John 7:1).

As we interrogate the text with the 5 W's and an H, we discover that...

"Jesus" answers the question, *"Who* is this about?"

"Was walking" answers the question, *"What* was He doing?"

"In Galilee, not Judea" answers the question, *"Where* was He walking?"

"Because the Jews were seeking to kill Him" tells us, *"Why* was He not in Judea?"

"After these things" tells us, *"When* was this action taking place?"

"What things?" The things that took place in the previous verses.

That is how you use the questioning technique of the 5 W's and an H. And the more you do it, the more it will become a habit, until asking these questions becomes second nature to you as you study God's awesome book.

Now, and this is important, don't think you have to find all 5 W's and an H every time you question a passage, because they're not always going to be there. For example, the verse above, John 7:1, did not answer an "H" question.

Simply read the text and answer all the 5 W's and an H questions you can.

Remember, every part of the entire process of inductive Bible study is based on asking who, what, when, where, why, and how kinds of questions. This is how vital the 5 W's and an H are!

Now, my friend, that you know the principles behind observation, let's move on to the process of observing the text. As you begin to do this, you're going to be excited by what you learn. And you'll probably find yourself saying, "I can't believe what I've seen all by myself!"

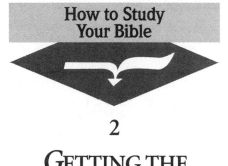

2

GETTING THE
BIG PICTURE

Although the Bible is a collection of 66 books written by many authors under the inspiration of the Holy Spirit, it was written one book at a time. And each book of the Bible has its own unique purpose and message.

If you've read much of the Bible, you know that many of the books cover similar material. Yet each book has its own place, value, and purpose in the whole counsel of God. So if you want to know your God intimately—to understand His mind, heart, ways, and how He wants you to live—you need to begin studying His Word book by book—one book at a time.

But with 66 books, where do you begin?

If you are new to the inductive study process, we suggest you begin with a short book.*

Once you've chosen a book, your first step is to get an overview of that book. An overview enables you to discover the overall context of the author's message. (Can you see why we say begin with a *short* book?)

---

*In our Precept Institute of Training, for example, we use 2 Timothy. It's short and it's convicting. After two days of study, people come away absolutely awed at what they've learned. In fact, they usually respond with something like this: "Why, oh why, didn't I know how to study this way sooner? I can't believe what I've learned! Why I learned more in two days than I've learned in the past _____ years."

The overview is Step 1 of the inductive process. It will give you the big picture and help you establish the framework of the book. Remember the puzzle illustration we used in the previous chapter? Well, the overview helps you find the corners and the straight edges, which in turn help you see the context of the book you're studying!

Getting an overview is like going up 3000 feet in an airplane to take pictures of some land you're thinking of purchasing. At 3000 feet you can't see the details of the property, but you can see the boundaries and the general lay of the land. Once you get those pictures, you'll zoom in to get a closer perspective of it acre by acre. Then eventually you'll land the plane, get out, and walk the land. As you do this, with the overview photos of the land in your hands, you'll gain a proper perspective of where you are and how everything on that property relates to the big picture.

An overview of the book helps you:

ﾆ see the message of the book as a whole, in its entirety

ﾆ gain an understanding of the author's purpose for writing

ﾆ identify the main theme(s) of the book

ﾆ become aware of the structure of the book

ﾆ understand the relationship of the verses and chapters to one another and to the book as a whole

ﾆ have a sound basis for accurate interpretation and correct application.

If this sounds like work, you are right. But, my friend, it really pays off. As a matter of fact, if you will put your energy here, it will make the rest of the process so much easier.

Now, in light of this fact, how do you get an overview of a book?

STEP ONE

Begin on Your Knees

Prayer is crucial to Bible study. When you get "into the plane"—when you start your overview—don't turn on the engines until you pray.

Since truth must be revealed by the Spirit of God, it follows that prayer must be an integral part of Bible study as you continually seek God's wisdom, counsel, and revelation. Give yourself time for the Holy Spirit to speak to your heart.

STEP TWO

Read and Re-read the Book

The more you read the book you have chosen to study, the more familiar you will become with it. There is no substitute for reading and prayerfully meditating on the Word of God. If you are studying a longer book, it may take several days to read the whole book through one time. But do it!

Your goal is to handle God's Word accurately. To do that, you've got to see the corners, find the straight edges, the boundaries. That is why it is easier to learn the inductive process with a shorter book.

The first time you read through the book, it may seem like a collection of verses that are barely related to one another. The more you read, however, the more you will see that all of those "isolated verses" really do belong together. Or when you read, you may come across some things which really puzzle you. Don't stop to try to figure them out. Now is not the time. Remember, first you look for the corners and straight pieces, then these difficult pieces will fall into place more easily.

As you read the book you are going to study, you'll also want to consciously...

STEP THREE

Identify the Type of Literature

The type of literature determines the way you will handle the text. For instance, Hebrew poetry (such as the Psalms) is different from the historical books (such as Kings and Chronicles), and the historical books are different from the epistles (such as 1 and 2 Timothy), both in style and content. History books give background and tell of real events and how God dealt with real people, but you don't build doctrine on historical events. Most of the doctrine for the church is contained in the epistles. So, recognizing the type of literature you're studying is important.

As you read through the book, determine which of the following best describes the book you're studying.

Is It Historical?

The book of Genesis sets forth the history of God's creation from the beginning of time, while the book of Judges records the period of Israel's history when the judges ruled. The book of Acts tells the history of the spread of the gospel and the beginning of the church.

Is It Biographical?

The book of Luke gives a chronological biography of our Lord Jesus Christ from His genealogy through His resurrection.

Is It Poetic?

The book of Psalms is Hebrew poetry.

Is It Proverbial?

The book of Proverbs, considered wisdom literature, is a compilation of concise sayings which set forth wisdom and instruction. Proverbs are not to be interpreted as prophecies or doctrines.

Is It Prophetic?

The book of Revelation describes itself as a book of prophecy. It tells of future events which are sure to come about.

Is It an Epistle (Letter)?

The book of 2 Timothy is a letter written to an individual. The book of Colossians is also a letter, but it is written to a church. The epistles contain most of the doctrine (teaching) for the church.

Is It a Combination*?*

Some books can be a combination of different types of literature. For example, the book of Daniel is both historical and prophetical. It tells of events past but also predicts future events.

Now, once you determine the type of literature, you need to...

STEP *F*OUR

Deal with the Text Objectively

Although we mentioned this before, it bears repeating, so listen carefully—be objective! Do not approach the Word of God subjectively, just to get something for yourself. Rather, come to the Word objectively, so God can teach you what you need to know. *Once you objectively see what God is saying, you'll know how that truth relates to you subjectively.*

Remember that context is identified by observing what is repeated over and over by the author. So in doing the overview of the book, you need to let the text speak for itself. One of the most effective tools for observing the text is the Observation Worksheet. You will learn how to use the Observation Worksheet in the next chapter.*

STEP *F*IVE

Use the 5 W's and an H

Be sure that you are reading with a purpose by interrogating the text with the 5 W's and an H. We covered this in the previous chapter, so you may want to turn back to that section and refresh your memory.

***Observation Worksheets** are the individual chapters of the book you're going to study, printed out on separate sheets. You'll find these in every Precept course, or you can make your own by simply typing out the text of the book you are studying, chapter by chapter. Double space the material and leave wide margins.

You will find an example of an Observation Worksheet in Appendix C on page 147.

Or better still, you may want to purchase the *New Inductive Study Bible*, which is designed specifically for this kind of study. The text is set in a single column with extra-wide margins for taking notes, and the *NISB* incorporates all the study charts and aids described in this book. It's an awesome Bible—absolutely unique—and invaluable for serious study. It's like having an entire Bible of Observation Worksheets.

STEP SIX

Discover Facts About People and Events

To discover the context of the book, begin by identifying the obvious. Depending on the type of literature you're studying, people and events are usually the most obvious and the easiest to identify.

Principle 1: Identify the Obvious Names

If, for example, you are studying one of Paul's epistles, you will first need to read through the book looking for and identifying the facts about the author, the recipients of the epistle, and any other people who are mentioned. If you're studying a different type of literature, such as one of the historical books, you will initially look for any mention of people in general as well as the specific events covered in the historical account. In prophetic literature the author may or may not be prominent, but people and events will be.

So keep all this in mind and, according to the type of literature, adapt what we're teaching you about seeing and identifying the obvious.

As you identify the facts about people and events, you begin to discern the historical and cultural context in which the author is writing. And this, of course, reflects on what he writes and how he writes.

Although God is the ultimate author of Scripture, He specifically chose certain human beings to write down His truths for Him (2 Timothy 3:16; 2 Peter 1:20-21). The books of the Bible are like light that comes through a prism. The prism separates the light, bringing out different colors and hues, yet it is still from one source—light. Therefore, many books of the Bible are also an expression of the human author: his background, his experiences, and his philosophy of life. Although the Bible is timeless, and every word divinely inspired, each book was written during a certain time period; therefore, each book is colored by the historical setting in which it was written. The political, social, philosophical, and even religious conditions of the times all came to bear on what was expressed on paper, yet without distorting or detracting from what God wanted written down for us.

To fully understand a book, all of these factors must be considered. This can be done by simply asking the who, what, when, where, why, and how kinds of questions about the people and events mentioned in the book.

You may have thought that the only way to understand the occasion and historical setting of a book was to read books about the Bible. But now you know that careful observation of the Word of God itself will reveal these facts to you. Isn't that exciting?

Now then, here are some practical steps to follow in order to identify the obvious.

STEP 1: Read through the text and mark in a distinctive way every mention of the author, the recipients, and other people. As you do, look for facts that tell you something about each person—facts that are unique to his or her identity and circumstances.

Do this on your Observation Worksheets (see the footnote on page 31) or in your Bible.

In a distinctive way, mark every mention of each person or group of people, as well as the pronouns (such as *I, me, my, we, us, our, who, whom, you, they,* and *their*) that refer to them.

Scripture can be marked distinctively in one of three ways:

- ✺ by coloring each use of the same word and its synonyms in one color or a combination of colors

- ✺ by drawing a diagram around that particular word to distinguish it from others*

---

*Be careful in your use of diagrams, as too many of them can become distracting when reading your Bible. I prefer to use colors and color combinations when possible and limit my diagrams. Colors enable me to spot the recurrence of words easily and quickly.

ᵔᵕ by combining color with a diagram. For instance, you could color "repent" yellow and then draw a diagram with it.

Whichever method you use, be consistent. Mark the text in this same manner throughout all the chapters of the book you are studying.

STEP 2: As you mark the references, ask the 5 W's and an H. For example:

> *Who* is the author?
>
> *Who* are the recipients?
>
> *Who* is this person?
>
> *What* does he tell you about himself?
>
> *What* are his circumstances?
>
> *Where* is he? Record any references to geographical locations. Also, turn to a map and locate these places. (The *New Inductive Study Bible* has maps right in the text.)
>
> *Why* is he there?
>
> *When* in his life is he writing?

These questions will give you clues to the **historical setting** of the book. Then ask...

> *Why* is he writing? *Why* are they doing this? *Why* is this being said to them?

As you ask these kinds of *Why* questions, the **purpose** of the book will become obvious. If the author doesn't give you a specific reason for writing, then the purpose will be revealed in other ways as you get more detailed in your observations.

> Ask, *What* does the author talk about the most? *What* are the people to do or not do?

As you ask these questions, the repeated emphasis in the book will show you the **theme** of the book.

STEP 3: Make a list of all you learn about the author and the people mentioned. This list will come from what you learned by marking the references and asking the 5 W's and an H and will give you valuable insights that will help you interpret the text properly.

Principle 2: Identify the Obvious Events

Are any events mentioned in the book? Remember, people and events are always the easiest to see; in fact, events may be more obvious than people. Therefore, as you read through the book, notice what events, if any, are mentioned in each chapter.

Once again, the type of literature, the purpose of the book, and the structure of the book can all be determining factors in what is the easiest to see.

For example, in the first 11 chapters of the book of Genesis, the focus is on four main events. Although people are mentioned, the events are the most obvious. Therefore, if you were studying this book, you would make a list of the event(s) described in each of these chapters.

The repetition of certain words and phrases shows that the emphasis in Genesis 1 is on the event of _God's creation of the world_. In Genesis 3 the primary events are _the temptation of Eve by the serpent_ and _man's choice to disobey God_. In Genesis 6–10 the event is _the flood_.

Marking the text and listing the facts surrounding these four main events will clearly show the emphasis in each of these first 11 chapters.

However, in Genesis 12–50 the emphasis switches from events to people—in fact, four major people: _Abraham, Isaac, Jacob,_ and _Joseph_. Therefore, you would mark the text and list the facts about these people, which would clearly show the primary emphasis in each chapter. Then, you'd look at the events of their lives and examine them in the light of the 5 W's and an H. Ask...

What is happening?

Where is it happening and _When_?

Who is involved?

What are the consequences of this event?

This process may appear laborious as you simply read through these instructions; however, once you actually put it into practice, you'll see how profitable it is.

But what do you do if the mention of people or events gives no real insight into the message of the book? For example, in the epistle of James the references to people and events do not really help you discover the context of the book. So where do you go next? You go to the next obvious thing: You look to see what subjects or topics the book deals with.

STEP SEVEN

Mark Key Words

As you read and re-read the text, you'll begin to notice that certain key words and/or phrases are repeated throughout the book, in a certain segment, or in several segments of the book.

Key words are words that are vital to understanding the meaning of the text. Like a key, they "unlock" the meaning of the text. A key word might be a noun, a descriptive word, or an action word that plays a part in conveying the author's message.

A key word or phrase is one which, when removed, leaves the passage devoid of meaning.

Often key words and phrases are repeated in order to convey the author's point or purpose for writing. They may be repeated throughout a chapter, a segment of a book, or the book as a whole.

> For example, in the book of 1 John the words "love," "sin," "abide," and "know" are repeated throughout the book, whereas "fellowship" is repeated only in chapter 1.

You'll want to mark each key word, along with synonyms and pronouns, in a distinctive way or color. A synonym is another word that means the same thing in the context being considered. A synonym is another way of saying the same thing.

For example, in the book of 2 Timothy, note these synonyms for "suffering":

- ❧ chains (1:16)

- ❧ hardship (2:3,9)

- ❧ persecutions (3:11)

The value of a distinctive marking system cannot be overestimated. Whichever way you choose to mark key words and their synonyms, mark each key word the same way every time you observe it throughout your study of the Word. Then, in future study, you will be able to track key subjects and quickly identify significant truths throughout the Scripture.

If you want to be consistent, list key words, symbols, and color codes on an index card and use it as a bookmark in your Bible. Be sure to mark pronouns (I, you, he, she, it, we, our, who, whom, which) and synonyms (words that have the same meaning in the context) the same way you mark the words to which they refer.

The more a word is repeated, the more obvious it becomes that the word represents a subject. The more that subject is repeated, the more obvious it becomes that the subject represents a theme in the book.

Key phrases and statements also give important repeated emphasis and/or show organization in a book.

For example, in the book of Judges the repetition of the statements "the sons of Israel again did evil," "there was no king in Israel, and...[man] did what was right in his own eyes" is key to understanding the message in Judges.

In the book of Haggai the phrase "the word of the Lord came [to]...Haggai" helps unlock the structure and purpose of the book.

It is imperative that you observe key words and phrases because they reveal the author's intended message, his intended emphasis, and how he will accomplish his purpose.

Every key word is a *Who* word or a *What* word or a *When* word or a *Where* word or a *Why* word or a *How* word. Therefore, every key word will answer one of these questions: *who, what, when, where, why,* or *how.*

KEY WORDS

SUBJECTS

THEME

Key words reveal the subjects. Subjects reveal the theme.

The more a word is repeated, the more obvious it becomes that the word represents a subject. The more that subject is repeated, the more obvious it becomes that the subject represents a theme in the book.

STEP *E*IGHT

Discern the Main Theme of the Book

Now that you've worked through the previous instructions, see if you can discern the statement that best summarizes the book (the summary statement).

As you do this, let the book reveal the theme to you. You do not have to "come up with" a book theme. It should be obvious. But if it's not, don't subjectively create a theme in your mind, based on emotion or *your* favorite passage. Discerning the **main theme or summary statement** should be an outgrowth of an objective evaluation of the repeated emphasis in the book. That is why, my friend, you need to give adequate time to the overview of the book.

The shorter the book, the easier it will be to discern the theme. So you may want to wait until you finish your *At a Glance Chart* (see step 9 on page 40) before you try to discern the theme.

Once you discern the theme (whenever that is—no rush!), look for a verse in the book that best covers or expresses that theme. That verse will become your **key verse** for the book.

Finally, write out a summary statement of the book. The very process of doing this will help crystallize the theme of the book, as well as seal it in your mind—and heart. Then in the future you'll know what book of the Bible you need to turn to in order to meet a specific need for truth or insight.

As you write out the theme, use as many key words from the text as possible and be as concise as you can.

> For example, in the Gospel of John the words "believe" and "life" are repeated over and over throughout the book. Then, at the end of the book, John clearly states his purpose:
>
>> "Therefore many other signs Jesus also performed in the presence of the disciples, which are not written in this book; but these have been written so that you may believe that Jesus is the Christ, the Son of God; and that believing you may have life in His name" (20:30-31).
>
> So, the key verse would be John 20:30-31. The summary statement for the Gospel of John should center on the author's purpose: Written that you might believe that Jesus Christ is the Son of God; and believing have life in His name.
>
> To look at another example: In the book of Hebrews the repeated emphasis is that Jesus is our great High Priest, so that could adequately serve as a summary statement for the book. The key verses could be Hebrews 4:14-16.

STEP NINE

Develop an At a Glance Chart

An At a Glance Chart is such a helpful tool for future reference, as well as giving you a quick synopsis of the book. Constructing such a chart will give you an invaluable visual overview of the book, which will enable you to see how the parts (the chapters) relate to the whole (book), which in turn will help you analyze the structure of the book you are studying.

In the Appendix you'll find a sample At a Glance Chart of the Gospel of John (see page 145). Stop and look at it now. As you study it, you'll see that you record the main theme of each chapter beside the chapter number on the chart.

You will construct a chart like this for each book you study.

If you have the _New Inductive Study Bible_, you'll find an At a Glance Chart at the end of each book of the Bible. After you fill it in, you'll always have that information with you. And you'll always be able to find where various truths are dealt with in the book. In long books this is an indispensable tool, for in a matter of seconds you can skim through the overall content of the book.

STEP TEN

Discover the Theme of Each Chapter

Do this the same way you came up with your book theme (see step 8).

A chapter theme should fall within two parameters: First, is it the main subject dealt with in that chapter? And second, does the theme relate to the overall book theme? If your choice of a theme or summary statement is truly the theme of the chapter, it will clearly relate to the book theme.

Once you have the theme, record it on the At a Glance Chart in the appropriate column. Do this for each chapter of the book.

Eventually, as you study the book chapter by chapter, you will choose a key verse for each chapter that reflects or provides the basis for what you have chosen as the chapter theme.

STEP ELEVEN

Identify Clearly Defined Segments

A segment division is a major division in a book, such as a group of verses or chapters that deal with the same subject, doctrine, person, place, or event.

Now, just as you don't subjectively create chapter themes, you don't subjectively create segment divisions. Rather, you discover them from the text. The context of the book determines the segment.

Not every book has clearly defined segments. However, if the book does divide into segments, you'll find that the number and type of divisions will vary according to the type of literature you are studying and according to the size of the book. A book might be divided (segmented) according to

∾ dates

∾ places

∾ topics

∾ doctrines

∾ reigns of kings

∾ major characters

∾ major events.

For instance, the book of Romans divides into two segments: chapters 1–11 are doctrinal; chapters 12–16 are practical.

In the book of Genesis, chapters 1–11 focus on four major events, and chapters 12–50 on four major characters.

In the book of Revelation, the divisions are clearly stated in Revelation 1:19:

> "Therefore write the things which you have seen, and the things which are, and the things which will take place after these things."

The segment divisions are: "the things which you have seen" (chapter 1); the "things which are" (chapters 2 and 3); and the "things which will take place after these things" (chapters 4–22). For segment divisions in the Gospel of John, look at the At a Glance Chart on page 145.

Discerning segment divisions requires time, practice, and a familiarity with the content of the book and the context in which it's laid out. Usually you will discover even more possible divisions after you have studied the book for a while. Therefore, the segment division part of your At a Glance Chart will be developed more completely as you become more familiar with a book.

Well, my friend, this is how you do an overview of a book. It's the most crucial part of all inductive study, for it sets the context for correctly interpreting and applying the text. Therefore, when you want to quickly review what you learned in this chapter, refer to Appendix A.

Now then, in the next section we'll take you step-by-step through the process of observing a book a chapter at a time. When we do, you will be excited about what you learn.

By the way, I'm so proud of you for making this effort to see truth for yourself. You will never regret it. God is going to open a whole new world of understanding to you...and you are going to be so grateful to Him.

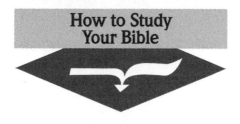
3

FOCUSING IN
ON THE DETAILS

*O*nce you've done your overview, you're off to a good start. Now you're ready to study the book chapter by chapter. Therefore, Step 2 in the process of inductive Bible study is the individual chapter study using the *Observation Worksheet* (see footnote on page 31).

To go back to the illustration we used in the previous chapter, you've finished surveying the property from the air. Now it's time to start surveying the land on foot, looking at the details. Or to return to our frog illustration, it's time to get the frog out of the pond!

In the overview, you discovered the basic framework of the book. Now your goal is to focus in on the more detailed observations of the content of each chapter.

STEP ONE

Remember to Pray

As you start observing the book one chapter at a time, remember truth is revealed by the Spirit, so begin with prayer and continue in prayer.

Luke 24:45 says, "Then He [Jesus] opened their minds to understand the Scriptures."

STEP *T*WO

Keep the Context in Mind

Don't forget that each chapter, and each truth contained in that chapter, must be considered in the context of the whole book, so remember all you learned in the overview. Keep it before you. It's foundational.

STEP *T*HREE

Does the Text Answer
Any of the 5 W's and an H?

Although the following may be a little repetitious, bear with me. Repetition and review are an integral part of the learning process. I will be brief, but let me emphasize this once again: Develop a questioning mindset. Remember to keep asking the 5 W's and an H as you read the text. Although the text may not necessarily have the answers to each question, it will still help you observe exactly what is being said. Ask questions such as...

Who spoke it? About *Whom? Who* are the major characters? *Who* are the people mentioned? To *Whom* is the author speaking?

What are the main events? *What* are the major ideas? *What* are the major teachings? *What* does the author talk about the most? *What* is his purpose in saying that?

When did this event take place? *When* will it happen? *When* did he say it?

Where was this done? *Where* was this said? *Where* will it happen?

Why was there a need for this to be written? *Why* was this mentioned? *Why* was it not mentioned?

Why was so much or so little space devoted to this particular event or teaching? *Why* was this reference mentioned?

How is it done? *How* is this truth illustrated?

Accurate answers from the text to these kinds of questions will help assure correct interpretation.

As you read, look only at the things that are obvious. If you focus on the obvious, ultimately those things that are obscure will become clearer.

Also, as you read, questions of interpretation will come to mind. When these questions arise, write them on another sheet of paper. Do not attempt to answer these questions until you have thoroughly observed the text.

STEP *F*OUR

Look For and Mark
Key Words and Phrases

At this point, before we go any further, let me suggest that you look at the sample Observation Worksheet on page 147. (If you have the *New Inductive Study Bible*, use it because the examples are in full color. Turn to *NISB* pages 19 and 21.) After looking at the Observation Worksheet, come back and continue reading. Then when you finish this segment, study it again. I don't know about you, but examples always help me. I'm the kind of person who learns better when someone *shows* me.*

Remember, a key word is a word the author uses repeatedly in a significant way, or a word which cannot be removed from the text without leaving it devoid of meaning. A key word might be a noun, a descriptive word, or an action word that plays a vital part in conveying the author's message.

You have already marked some key words during the overview. Now, continue the process on the same Observation Worksheet, building upon what you discovered in the overview. "Walking through the text" at a slower pace, you will see other key words and phrases that you didn't notice before.

As with the overview, when you discover more key words and phrases, you will want to mark them in a distinctive way on your Observation Worksheet. You can do this either by coloring each use of the same word and its synonyms and pronouns in one color or by drawing a distinctive diagram around that particular word to distinguish it from others. Remember, colors are preferable. Eight-color Pentel pencils are available for this purpose at most Christian bookstores. They are sold in conjunction with the *New Inductive Study Bible.*

You are now looking for words that are key to this particular chapter, even though they may not be key in any other chapter.

Every key word is a *who, what, when, where, why,* or *how* word.

At this stage, mark only one key word at a time as you read through the chapter. This means every time you mark a different key word, you'll read through the chapter again. Thus, if you are marking five key words, you will read the chapter five times.

Marking the text in this way helps you slow down and soak in the content of the chapter, letting the Holy Spirit minister truth to you as you read and re-read the Word. As a matter of fact, when you read Scripture over and over again you will find yourself automatically remembering it. You will also find yourself beginning to hide God's

---

*If you would like to attend a hands-on How to Study Your Bible Workshop in an area near you, write Precept Ministries, P.O. Box 182218, Chattanooga, TN 37422.

Word in your heart, rather than just skimming along making colorful marks on paper. The important thing is not the marking, but what you learn by marking that word.

All references to God the Father, the Son, or the Holy Spirit should be considered key words. Depending on how frequently they occur in the text, you may or may not want to mark them. You may simply want to make a mental note of them. Whichever way you choose, as you mark or note references to the Father, Son, and Spirit, ask the 5 W's and an H kinds of questions regarding the text. For instance...

Who is this—God, Jesus, or the Holy Spirit?

What is this telling me about God, Jesus, or the Holy Spirit?

Why is this mentioned?

Be careful that you don't just go through this marking process by rote, mindlessly marking the words. Be sure that you are really reading the text and thinking about it so that you comprehend all it has to teach you about God, Jesus, and the Holy Spirit.

The value of marking and evaluating the references to God, Jesus, and the Holy Spirit is that you begin to build a firm foundation in your understanding of the Trinity—understanding the differences between the person and work of God, Jesus, and the Holy Spirit as the Bible defines them and understanding the similarities.

STEP *Five*

List What You Learned About Each Word

A list is a compilation of every fact given about a particular word, subject, person, place, or event in a single chapter. These facts are answers to the 5 W's and an H.

Put each list on a separate sheet of paper, heading it with the key word. (After you have refined your lists, you can transfer them to the margin of your Bible or worksheet.) For example, if you made a list on "God" from 2 Timothy 1, it would look something like this:

God
1. made Paul an apostle by His will (v. 1)
2. gives grace, mercy, and peace (v. 2)
3. is the Father (v. 2)
4. is thanked and served (v. 3)
5. gives gifts (v. 6)
6. doesn't give spirit of timidity (v. 7)
7. gives spirit of power, love, and
   discipline (v. 7)
8. gives power for suffering (v. 8)
9. saved us (v. 9)
10. called us (v. 9)

When you evaluate this list, you will notice that the subject of salvation has come up (2 Timothy tells us that God saved us, God called us, etc.). With this, you have the basis for another list, which brings us to an important principle: As you observe the text, you're going to stumble on topical lists, such as this one on the subject of salvation.

Salvation
1. God saved us (v. 9)
2. God called us with a holy calling (v. 9)
   – not according to our works (v. 9)
   – according to His purpose and grace (v. 9)
3. was granted to us in Christ Jesus (v. 9)
   – from all eternity (v. 9)
4. now has been revealed by the appearing
   of our Savior Christ Jesus (v. 10)

Be on the alert for topical lists. As you can see from the list on salvation, remember that not all lists of truths are formed from key words. However, key words are usually the basis for a list.

❧
STEP SIX

Look for Contrasts, Comparisons, Terms of Conclusion, and Expressions of Time

Contrasting Words and Phrases

A **contrast** is an evaluation of things that are different or opposite in the context being viewed. Many times, contrast is noted by the word "but."

> For example, note the contrast between what God has and hasn't given us in 2 Timothy 1:7:

> > "For God has not given us a spirit of timidity, **but** of power and love and discipline."

However, as you look for contrasts, remember the contrast is not necessarily between the actual words. It can be a contrast within the thought or body of truth conveyed by the words in that particular context.

> For example, the words "night" and "day" seem like an obvious contrast. Yet in the following context, they are not. In 2 Timothy 1:3 Paul says:

> > "I constantly remember you in my prayers night and day."

This is not a contrast, but shows that Paul prays during both times.

> However, in 1 Thessalonians 5:5 he uses night and day to contrast the sons of light and the sons of darkness:

> > "For you are all sons of light and sons of day. We are not of night nor of darkness."

Therefore, make sure that you are not just marking contrasting words, but contrasting thoughts.

Many times the words "but," "however," or "nevertheless" show a contrast. When you see those words, read the context to see if two different things are being compared.

You can make a mental note of the contrast, or if you prefer, you can note the contrast in the margin of your Bible or right in the text like this:

> 1:7 For God has not given us a spirit of timidity, but of power and love and discipline.

What truth is being revealed through the contrast? What point is the author making through the contrast? That's what you want to discern.

Words of Comparison

A **comparison** always refers to things that are similar or alike. Many times the words "like" and "as" signify a comparison.

Determine, if possible, what truth is being revealed through the comparison. Then note the comparison in the margin or mark it in the text. For example in 2 Timothy:

> 2:3 Suffer hardship with me, as a good soldier of Christ Jesus.

Expressions of Time

Words such as "then," "after this," "until," and "when" show **timing or sequence of events**. They answer the question, *When?*

Make a note in the text of any reference to time. As you mark these expressions of time, observe what you learn from noting "when" something occurs, which can be crucial when it comes to interpreting the text. This is especially seen in passages like Matthew 24:15-31, where the "whens" and "thens" lay out the sequence of events.

Expressions of time can be marked by drawing a clock in the margin or by simply drawing a clock face over the word itself. Personally, I also color my clock green so I can spot it even more easily.

Terms of Conclusion and Result

Words such as "therefore," "for," "so that," and "for this reason" indicate that **a conclusion or summary** is being made or that **a result** is being stated. Therefore, watch for such terms!

You may want to underline these as you observe them in the text. Here is an example from 2 Timothy:

> 1:7 For God has not given us a spirit of timidity, but of power and love and discipline.

> 1:8 Therefore do not be ashamed of the testimony of our Lord or of me His prisoner, but join with me in suffering for the gospel according to the power of God.

The conclusion? Because God has given us a spirit of power, love, and discipline—rather than timidity—we are not to be ashamed of the testimony of our Lord.

Other terms of conclusion or result in this chapter are:

> 1:4 longing to see you...so that I may be filled with joy.

> 1:6 for this reason I remind you....(What reason? Verse 5 tells us: "because of the sincere faith within you.")

> 1:12 For this reason I also suffer these things....(What reason? Verse 11 says: because "I was appointed a preacher and an apostle and a teacher.")

This, friend, is how to watch for contrasts, comparisons, expressions of time, and terms of conclusion or result.

STEP SEVEN

With Historical or Biographical Books:

If you are studying historical or biographical books, it is helpful to record the following:

- ∿ The location and/or timing of the opening of the chapter. You can put this information just above the first verse on your Observation Worksheet, if you're using one, or in the margin of your Bible.

∾ Any significant changes in location or time as they occur in the chapter.

∾ Major characters, doctrines, and events covered in the chapter. Record this information at the end of your Observation Worksheet or on a sheet of paper under each category.

Major Characters   **Major Doctrines**   **Major Events**

These summations will not only help you in the future, but will serve to help you observe and analyze exactly what is in that chapter.

If you will maintain a prayerful, teachable spirit as you do your observations, you will find that the Holy Spirit will use all of this to speak to you and to reveal to you precious treasures of truth.

STEP EIGHT

Check Chapter Theme

Now that you've come this far, simply check out the chapter theme you came up with when you did your overview. Does it adequately describe the main teaching of the chapter? If so, congratulate yourself. If not, change it—then congratulate yourself for seeing your need to make the change.

STEP NINE

Develop Memorable Paragraph Themes

Some people like to do paragraph themes or write out statements that summarize the content of each paragraph in the chapter. Although this means more work on your part, the very process of doing this will give you an even better grasp of the text.

Just as the book theme is supported by and carried out by the chapter themes in the overview, here the chapter theme is supported by and carried out by the paragraph themes.

From the Whole to the Parts

Remember that *at every point you have gone from the whole to the parts.* You began by looking at the whole book, getting an overview of the book, discovering its theme. Then you moved to its parts, the chapters, discovering the chapter themes.

Now you are moving from the whole chapter to its parts, the paragraphs and their themes.

The paragraph divisions in your Bible are shown by an indentation at the start of a paragraph, or the paragraph symbol, or boldface type for the verse number of the first verse of the paragraph, or some combination of these. Check to see what method your Bible publisher has used.

What can make doing paragraph themes somewhat difficult is that the chapter and paragraph divisions are man-made. They even differ from translation to translation.

Although there might be differences in paragraph divisions, however, it doesn't change the author's original flow of thought.

Let the Paragraph Talk

If you do paragraph themes, use the same rules you used for the book and chapter themes. Just remember, you do not ever have to "come up with" a paragraph theme or summary statement. All you have to do is let the paragraph reveal the theme to you, and then analyze the contents of the paragraph to discover the best summary statement.

Evaluate the truths in the paragraph and, using words from the text, summarize the content of the paragraph in as few words as possible.

Your theme needs to be descriptive of the paragraph's theme and yet distinctive from the other chapter or paragraph themes.

Choose the paragraph themes in light of the chapter theme.

When you do paragraph themes, it is best to write them in the left margin of your Observation Worksheet opposite the paragraph.

Often in an epistle, the first paragraph will just be a salutation to the book.

For example, a possible way to describe the first paragraph in 2 Timothy 1 would be: "From Paul to Timothy" or "To Timothy."

The following outline shows you the flow of thought all the way from the book theme to the paragraph theme.

Book—theme

    Chapter 1—theme

        Paragraph 1—theme

        Paragraph 2—theme

        Paragraph 3—theme

    Chapter 2—theme

        Paragraph 1—theme

        Paragraph 2—theme

    Chapter 3—theme

        Paragraph 1—theme

        Paragraph 2—theme

        Paragraph 3—theme

        Paragraph 4—theme

If you carry out this process throughout the book you are studying, you will have a comprehensive outline of the book comprised of the main themes of the paragraphs and chapters of the book. Take a look at the detailed outline of 2 Timothy in Chapter 13, "Outlining—Just the Bare Facts" on pages 123–128.

When you do the overview, you will have more questions than answers, since you are only getting the big picture. As you do a more detailed chapter study, you will find many of those answers.

However, even if you haven't, keep your list before you. Resist the temptation to go to your commentaries until you've done some more personal work with the text. That's what we'll look at next.

Are you concerned, my friend, that you are not going to come up with the right answers? Relax; don't panic. These are skills that are developed through repeated use until they become second nature. You do the best you can and God will meet you there. He knows your heart and will honor your diligence. Remember, those who succeed are those who determine to keep on keeping on until they learn. I always tell my students, "Hangeth, thou, in there!"

～～～～～

Part Two

INTERPRETATION

Discover What It Means!

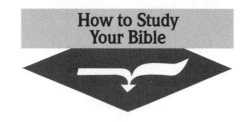
4

THE SEARCH FOR MEANING

ᲪᲙᲫᲙᲫᲙ

*H*ave you ever heard someone walk out of a teaching session
and say, "That teacher has done his homework!"?

What did they mean? They meant that the teacher really knew the
subject—he or she had done a thorough job of preparation before
teaching the class.

Well, friend, when you have done your observations, as laid out in
the first portion of this book, you have "done your homework."

You have done the imperative: You've observed the text, and in
doing so you have laid the essential foundation for understanding what
the book you are studying is all about. You have not neglected the one
thing which is needful for accurately interpreting the Word of God:
observation. You have overviewed the text so that you understand its
context. You have explored it chapter by chapter, paragraph by paragraph, verse by verse so that you know what it says. And look at how
much you have learned in the process!

You've landed the plane and walked through the land on foot, cov-
ering every inch. But there's more.

Now it is time to do a careful analysis of the earth itself, the vegeta-
tion, the soil. You want to know why the land produces what it does,
the way it does, and what the soil is like.

In inductive Bible study, that's what we call the discipline of interpretation. And that's the point we're at now.

You know what the book you are studying says, but you still have questions because you still don't know what certain things mean. And you want a correct analysis. You want truth—nothing less. You want to handle God's Word accurately. You want to please God, to have His approval for your stewardship of His Word. Plus, you know that if you are going to live life the way it should be lived, it has to be lived in truth.

So how does a child of God go about making sure that he or she really knows what the Word means? Well, as we have already said, you have done the essential—observation—and now you build from there.

Let us give you some basic principles to follow when you interpret the Word of God. Then we'll follow those principles with specific instructions on how to better understand and analyze the text through word studies, understanding figures of speech and handling them properly, knowing how to deal with prophetic passages, etc. All these will help you, so to speak, examine the soil of God's Word.

So first, let's look at seven basic principles which will help you interpret the Bible accurately.

Principle 1: Remember that context rules.

By now you're familiar with context. You know the word "context" means "that which goes with the text." When you interpret anything—a word, a verse, a teaching—it must always be considered in the light of...

    ∾ the surrounding verses and chapters

    ∾ the book in which it is found

    ∾ the entire Word of God.

Therefore, as you seek to know what something means, ask yourself,

    ∾ Is my interpretation of a particular section of Scripture consistent with the theme, purpose, and structure of the book in which it is found?

∾ Is my interpretation consistent with other Scriptures about the same subject, or is there a glaring difference?

∾ Am I considering the historical and cultural context of what is being said?

For example, 2 Timothy 2:16 says, "...avoid worldly *and* empty chatter...." Does this mean that Christians should not tell funny stories or talk about the mundane things of the world? A careful examination of the text will shed light on the meaning of this statement and show that the subject being considered is the gospel and the need to handle it accurately, not whether or not a Christian should tell funny stories.

Never take a Scripture out of its context to make it say something that is contrary to the text. Even if what you might say would be considered "a blessing to that person," always handle the Word objectively; then subjective blessings will be based on truth, not error. Discover what the author is saying—remembering that the ultimate author is God—and do not add to his meaning.

Principle 2: Always seek the full counsel of the Word of God.

When you know God's Word thoroughly, you will not accept a teaching simply because someone has used one or two isolated verses to support that teaching. Those verses could have been taken out of context, or other important passages might have been overlooked or ignored—passages that might have led to a different understanding.

As you read the Bible regularly and extensively and become more familiar with the whole counsel of God's Word, you will be able to discern whether a teaching is biblical or not.*

For example, in John 15:7 Jesus says, "...ask whatever you wish, and it will be done for you." Does that mean that you can ask *anything* at all from God and He will give it to you? The answer is no! The Bible has much more to teach about prayer than just that one statement,

---

*The International Inductive Study Series is especially designed for this purpose and is ideal material for Sunday school, small group studies, or personal study. This series, published by Harvest House Publishers, is a survey course, while Precept Upon Precept Bible Studies provide in-depth studies of various books of the Bible.

such as asking according to God's will (1 John 5:14) and asking with the right motivation (James 4:3). These Scriptures and more must be considered when evaluating this subject.

Saturate yourself in the Word of God; it is your safeguard against wrong doctrine.

Principle 3: Remember that Scripture will never contradict Scripture.

The best interpreter of Scripture is Scripture. Remember, all Scripture is inspired by God; it is God-breathed. Therefore, Scripture will never contradict itself. If it appears to, then your interpretation of at least one passage is incomplete or wrong.

The Bible contains all the truth you will ever need for any situation in life (2 Peter 1:3). Sometimes, however, you may find it difficult to reconcile two seemingly contradictory truths taught in Scripture—for example, the sovereignty of God and the responsibility of man. It's hard to reconcile these two teachings in our minds; they don't seem to fit together. Yet the Bible clearly teaches both. What do you do? Choose what you've been taught or what you'd like to believe or what falls in line with your concept of God? No—you can't do any of these and deal with the Scriptures with integrity. When two or more truths that are clearly taught in the Word seem to be in conflict, remember that you as a human have a finite mind. Don't take a teaching to an extreme that God doesn't in order to reconcile it in your understanding! Let God say what He says without trying to correct or explain Him. Remember, He's God—you're man. Simply humble your heart in faith and believe what God says, even if you can't understand or reconcile it at the moment.

Principle 4: Do not base your doctrine on an obscure passage of Scripture.

An obscure passage is one in which the meaning is not easily understood. Because these passages are difficult to understand even when proper principles of interpretation are used, they should not be used as a basis for establishing doctrine. Your doctrine should be based on the clear repeated teachings in the Scripture.

An example of this type of obscurity is found in 1 Corinthians 15:29 where the question is asked, "...what will those do who are baptized for the dead?" Does this mean we are to be baptized for the dead? Is this a teaching that should become a doctrine for believers to practice? No, this is not a doctrinal statement. In fact, the meaning here is not clear. So without clear understanding and other scriptural support, it should not be considered a doctrine and applied to your life.

Principle 5: Interpret Scripture literally.

The Bible is not a book of mysticism. God has spoken to us through His Word that we might know His truth. Therefore, take the Word of God at face value, in its natural, normal sense. Look first for the clear teaching of Scripture, not some hidden meaning. Understand and recognize figures of speech and interpret them accordingly.

Consider what is being said in the light of its literary style. For example, you will find more similes and metaphors in poetical and prophetic literature than in historical or biographical books.

Proverbs are wise sayings that are generally true to life. We read them and say, "Yes, that's life." However, these maxims cannot be interpreted as prophecies, nor can they be held as absolute promises for all people for all times. For example, Proverbs says that a man's enemies will be at peace with him when his ways please the Lord. At one level, you can accept this as a valid proverb which often proves to be true to life. Yet overall, you know that this is not always true. For example, Jesus' enemies were not at peace with Him, even though He did only those things which pleased the Father.

In the chapters that follow there are explanations that shed light on many of the styles and literary devices used by the writers of Scripture. Interpret portions of Scripture according to their literary style.

Principle 6: Look for the author's intended meaning of the passage.

Always try to understand what the author had in mind when you interpret a portion of the Bible. Don't twist verses to support a meaning that is not clearly taught. Let the passage speak for itself.

Judges 6, for example, tells the story of Gideon's fleece. However, this particular chapter is not teaching us that the way to know God's will for sure is to "put out a fleece." Judges records events that happened during a certain period in Israel's history, and this chapter is simply a historical account of what Gideon did when he was afraid. There are no instructions anywhere in the Bible that suggest that putting out a fleece is the proper procedure to follow in determining what the will of God is.

When we ascribe meaning to a passage that the author did not intend, then we are assuming an authority equivalent to that of the author. And the author of all Scripture is really God.

Principle 7: Check your conclusions by using reliable commentaries.

Up to this point in the inductive study process you have been asked not to read commentaries. But commentaries do have their place.

Commentaries come in several varieties. Some are strictly devotional and are probably not what you want to use for in-depth Bible study. Some commentaries are analytical and, therefore, more helpful in this type of study.

It is vital to use commentaries that examine the text with integrity and give explanations and comments that are in keeping with the context. Also, you will want to use commentaries that have been written by scholars who are known to hold to the inerrancy of the Word. If possible, check out more than one commentator on the book you are studying so you can weigh various interpretations.

As you consult these various commentaries, remember that no one person has a corner on all the truth. You may disagree with the writer on one thing and agree on another, but don't discount all an author says just because you don't see everything the same way. And don't believe it just because a godly person who is a scholar has said, "This is what it means." Check out the interpretation according to the inductive principles you have been given. Make sure the *commentator* is handling the text correctly. Some commentators simply borrow from others without doing the basics of inductive study themselves. Error is propagated when we don't bring everything we believe back to the

Be very wary if in your study you find something that no one else has ever seen before. God probably would not blind godly men to truth for almost 2,000 years and suddenly reveal it to you.

plumb line of God's Word. So bring all you read up against all you've seen as you have observed the text yourself. If you will do this, then you can properly handle the teachings of others.

In fact, teachers and commentaries can be a safeguard for you in your own interpretation. Be very wary if in your study you find something that no one else has ever seen before. God probably would not blind godly men to truth for almost 2,000 years and suddenly reveal it to you.

Now, here's a checklist to use when drawing conclusions from your interpretation:

- ෨ Do not contradict the context of the book, chapter, or passage you are studying. Context is always king in interpretation; it rules. A text out of context is a pretext.

- ෨ Do not violate the general theme of the book you are studying.

- ෨ Check to see if your conclusions are in accordance or agreement with what the author said in other books of his writing.

- ෨ Make sure your conclusions do not violate other biblical truths.

- ෨ Make sure your conclusions are not "prejudiced" to one particular doctrine or school of theology, as this often distorts one's interpretation.

Well, my friend, are you excited about what you are learning—or a little overwhelmed because of the work involved? Remember, I told you that this method is not easy, but it is more than worthwhile for those who are willing to discipline themselves for the purpose of godliness.

By the way, if you want a 13-week study that will take you by the hand and help you put all these skills into practice in a simple but powerful way, you might try my book *God, Are You There?* (Harvest House Publishers).

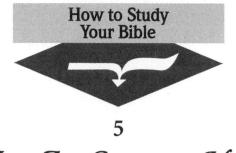

5

IT'S ALL GREEK TO ME!

∽∾∽∾∽∾

*H*ave you ever heard anyone say, "I don't know—it's all Greek to me!"? Well, whether you know Greek or not, understanding the Word of God doesn't have to be "Greek to you." Whether you know Greek or not, understanding some of the ways the Greek language works can explain a lot to you that in turn can help you fine-tune your interpretation of the Word.

Beloved, look at all you have learned just by studying God's Word for yourself. You are to be commended. And I urge you to continue. Truly the best is yet to come.

One of the study techniques available to help you fine-tune your understanding of Scripture is "word study," which is the study of words in the original languages of the Old and New Testaments. The Bible was originally written in Hebrew, Greek, and some Aramaic, and then translated into English and other languages. In the process of interpretation, therefore, it often helps to go back to the original languages to gain greater insight and/or clarification. Word studies are Step 3 of the process of inductive study.

The Old Testament was written primarily in Hebrew with some Aramaic and was then translated into Koine Greek about 100 B.C. This translation is referred to as the LXX or the Septuagint. Many New Testament writers quoted from the Septuagint when they wrote their "books."

The New Testament was written in Koine Greek. Koine (which means "common") Greek was the legal language in the lands where the books of the New Testament were written and was still in use during the time of the Roman Empire. Although Koine Greek fell into disuse after about A.D. 300, scholars have produced a number of Greek study tools for the English reader of the Bible that help us understand what the original authors meant to convey.

Why is it necessary to do word studies when we have many good translations of the ancient biblical manuscripts? Because although translations of the Bible are usually done by teams that operate by consensus to find the best equivalent word, it's often impossible to find an exact match in meaning from one language to another. Also, sometimes there is a difference between the way we understand an English word and the way the translators understood it. And sometimes it's hard to convey the tense, voice, and mood of verbs when you translate them into another language.

In many instances, therefore, you need to go back to the original language to get the full meaning of a word or the full import of a verb— which in turn can be a valuable tool in understanding the text or a difficult teaching. Going back to the original language also can help you know where words are used, how they are used, and by whom. So in word studies, it is not always just a matter of referring back to the original language, but also looking to see how the word is used in other Scriptures.

The purpose for doing word studies
is to understand the meaning of a word or words
in the context you are studying.

Once you have discovered the original meaning or use of a word, you can take the definition and use of the word back into the text to see how they enhance your understanding of the passage. Sometimes, of course, you'll see that the translation is so clear you won't see anything new.

And what if you don't know Hebrew, Greek, and Aramaic? Well, a variety of word study tools are available today, and in this section we will introduce you to some of the most accessible ones, designed for the person who does not necessarily know the original languages. (There are many other tools available, but they require knowledge of Hebrew or Greek.)

First Essential: An Exhaustive Concordance

An exhaustive concordance shows where each word in a particular translation is used throughout Scripture. Each concordance is keyed to the English words in a particular translation of the Bible (for example, the KJV, NASB, NIV). An exhaustive concordance is one that shows *all* the references to all the words in a given translation.

For example, if you want to know where else the word "guard" (2 Timothy 1:14) is used in the New American Standard Bible, you look up that word in your NASB concordance, and it will list every instance where the word "guard" appears in that translation of the Bible.

In choosing a concordance you should select one that is keyed to the version (translation) of the Bible that you use for study. Another essential feature your concordance should have is the means to show you the original language word from which the English language word was translated (Greek for the New Testament and Hebrew or Aramaic for the Old Testament).

There are several exhaustive concordances available, among which are *Strong's Exhaustive Concordance* and the *New American Standard Exhaustive Concordance*. Strong's is keyed to the King James Version of the Bible (often abbreviated KJV or AV, which stands for Authorized Version). Both these concordances work in an identical manner, although there are minor differences, as you will see in the examples in Appendix D.

69

Strong's and the *New American Standard Exhaustive Concordance* are divided into two sections: the concordance, which is located in the front, and the Hebrew and Greek dictionaries, which are located in the back. The concordance section has the Scripture reference for every word. The dictionaries contain the Hebrew (O.T.) and Greek (N.T.) words and their definitions. Dictionary entries give definitions and other information for every word from which the English was translated.

How to use the concordance:

STEP 1: Look up the English word in the concordance, find the Scripture reference where that word is used, then find the number code (these numbers are the same in both Strong's and the New American Standard concordances).

STEP 2: Turn to the back of the concordance to either the Greek or Hebrew dictionary, depending on whether you are studying a passage from the New or Old Testament (Hebrew for the O.T. and Greek for the N.T.).

STEP 3: Find the number and the corresponding Greek or Hebrew word. The definition for that word will be in italic type, before the colon and dash (:—).

In Appendix D you'll find a detailed example on how to use a concordance on page 149.

Second Essential: An Expository Dictionary

The second tool that is essential to word studies is an expository dictionary of biblical words. An expository dictionary gives more expansive definitions than those available in the concordance dictionaries.

Although there are a number of good expository dictionaries available, we recommend the following: Spiros Zodhiates, *The Complete Word Study Dictionary: New Testament;* W. E. Vine, *Vine's Complete Expository Dictionary of Old and New Testament Words;* Laird Harris, *Theological Wordbook of the Old Testament.* Although the work by Harris is complicated, it may be worthwhile in your study.

If you are using Zodhiates' dictionary, look up the Strong's number from your concordance and read the corresponding article in the dictionary. If you are using Vine's, which is keyed to the King James Version, look up the KJV English word, then under it find the article on the Greek or Hebrew word you found in the concordance.

In Appendix D you will find a detailed explanation of how to use different kinds of expository dictionaries on page 154.

After you have determined the meaning from your exhaustive concordance and expository dictionary, then take that definition back to the verse you are studying and see if it clarifies your understanding of the text.

Remember, the purpose of doing a word study is to learn more about the passage based on a fuller understanding of the meaning of a word from the original language of Hebrew or Greek.

Another Helpful Tool:
Understanding How Words Work

In addition to the simple step of discovering the meaning of the Greek or Hebrew word from which the English was translated, much can be learned from knowing something of the parts of speech of the original language, especially in the Greek.

Because verbs express action, they are often the most significant element in the expression of thought. Therefore, *understanding the Greek verb can be an important key to a correct interpretation and application of Scripture.*

Part of the beauty of the Greek language is that the construction of the verbs clearly shows who does the action, whether the statement is a command or a suggestion, and whether the passage is speaking of reality or possibility. The major features of Greek verbs are tense, voice, and mood. By thinking through a simple, concise explanation of tense, voice, and mood, new vistas of insight will be opened to you.

Remember, however, context is the most important key to correct interpretation and application, since the Greek words get their meaning from the context. Context is king!

In Appendix E you will find an explanation of the tense, voice, and mood of Greek verbs that will help those who do not know Greek but want a better understanding of the implications of the kind of action indicated by the verbs. Also included in Appendix F is an explanation of some word study tools that are available for this level of word study. Keep in mind that the explanation is a simplified summary of a complex subject. The purpose of this information is to give you an overview of terms that are frequently used in the more technical commentaries. (All this information is also available in the *New Inductive Study Bible*. If you have that Bible, this information is always immediately accessible, whether you're studying or teaching.)

As we say all this about Greek verbs, we realize it is inappropriate to think that a short section in a book like this will be sufficient to replace the knowledge one might gain by studying the Greek language in a formal educational setting. In trying to simplify the Greek to suit the purposes of this book, we believe we cannot do justice to the subject. Therefore, we will restrict the material in the appendixes to only the necessary explanation of the value of using various Greek study tools in understanding the Scripture and introductions to the use of one or two of the easiest.

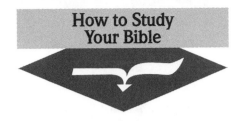
6

LET SCRIPTURE
INTERPRET SCRIPTURE

~~~~~~~

*T*he Bible is one revelation without contradiction. Therefore, when studying any particular book of the Bible, ultimately that book must be evaluated in the light of the entire Bible. Because context rules in interpretation, both the immediate context of the chapter and book must be considered, as well as the remote context of the whole Bible.

God usually does not exhaust a subject in just one book; He has chosen to give us bits and pieces of truths throughout His Word. Therefore, to get the whole counsel of the Word of God, the process of interpretation often encompasses related passages from other books of the Bible (Acts 20:27). To be sure that you accurately handle His Word, you need to study all of the places in the Bible where a subject is taught. And this is where cross-references come in.

A cross-reference is a reference to another Scripture that supports, illumines, or amplifies the Scripture you are studying. In other words, when you do cross-referencing, you compare Scripture with Scripture.

Because Scripture will never contradict Scripture, the best interpretation for Scripture is other Scripture. Therefore, if there seems to be a discrepancy when you compare Scripture, check your interpretation, for somewhere you have gone amiss.

*To be sure that you accurately handle His Word,
you need to study all of the places in the Bible
where a subject is taught.*

How Do You Cross-Reference Scripture?

STEP 1: The first place you can begin is with a concordance and/or a study tool that will show you other places where the same Hebrew or Greek word is used, or where the same subject is referred to: for example, baptism, gifts of the Spirit, the second coming of Christ.

For instance you could use the Strong's or NASB concordance, Dr. Zodhiates' *Complete Word Study New Testament,* or Smith's *Greek-English Concordance to the New Testament,* or a topical Bible, or the reference system in your Bible (with discretion).

List each cross-reference for the word or subject you want to study. (Remember: an exhaustive concordance lists every reference for every word in the Bible.)

STEP 2: Then in your Bible turn to each of the cross-references and study the context of each cross-reference. Remember, a Scripture cannot be wrenched out of its context. If you do, the text becomes a pretext.

STEP 3: When you find a cross-reference that illuminates the Scriptures you are studying, you might want to make note of it in the margin of your Bible next to the appropriate Scripture. In this way, you can develop your own cross-referencing system in your Bible. (This is another reason you should have a Bible with adequate margins. They're larger and weigh more, but they're well worth it.)

STEP 4: In the course of checking these cross-references, you'll probably notice that you will read quite a few passages that don't really pertain to the subject you are studying. This occurs because what you have done is a word cross-reference, and although the same word is used in these references, it might not pertain to your study focus, or even if it does, it might not help your understanding.

An Example of the Need to Cross-Reference

In 2 Timothy, Paul calls Timothy his beloved son (1:2). Paul also mentions Timothy's mother, Eunice, and his grandmother, Lois. So, a logical question is, "Why does Paul call Timothy his 'beloved son'? Was he Paul's physical son or his spiritual son?" From the text of 2 Timothy it is not clear; this book does not tell us whether or not Eunice was Paul's wife and Lois his mother-in-law.

STEP 1: We first go to the concordance and look up "Timothy" and see what Scripture references are given. The list in the concordance shows us there are 24 verses in the Bible that mention Timothy.

STEP 2: Next, we look up these cross-references in our Bible and read them to see what we can glean regarding Paul's reference to Timothy as his beloved son.

STEP 3: Some of the most helpful cross-references are Acts 16:1; 1 Corinthians 4:17; and Philippians 2:19. As we check these, we want to answer the following questions:

> *What* do these Scriptures reveal about Timothy's family? Is Paul his physical father? Is Paul his spiritual father? Is there any record that tells you that Paul led Timothy to the Lord?

> *When* did Paul and Timothy meet? Was it before Timothy came to the Lord or was it after?

> *What* happened after they met?

> Can you tell from these passages *Why* Paul would call Timothy his son?

STEP 4: From checking these cross-references we discover that Timothy was already a disciple when Paul met him. He was the son of a

Jewish woman who was a believer, and his father was a Greek. Timothy was well spoken of by the brethren. Paul wanted to take Timothy with him on his missionary journey. He had a kindred spirit with Paul and had served with Paul in the furtherance of the gospel, like a child serving with his father. Thus, Timothy was Paul's spiritual son, not his physical son.

Cross-Referencing Other Subjects

What if the subject you need to cross-reference is not a proper name, but just a word from the text such as a noun, verb, adjective, or adverb? What would you need to keep in mind?

When looking in the concordance, make sure that the same number, the same Greek word, is used in the cross-reference you choose to check. For example, the KJV translates several different Greek words into the same English word "suffer." To cross-reference the same Greek word, you must be sure you are dealing with the same number.

Remember, as you check cross-references, that you are going from the context of the book you're studying to the whole Bible, the larger context. You are allowing Scripture to interpret Scripture. And nothing is safer!

Oh, my friend, get to know the whole counsel of the Word of God. Such familiarity with the Word is invaluable.*

---

* The International Inductive Study Series (Harvest House Publishers) is ideal for this. In relatively short order and at an affordable cost, you not only survey one or several books of the Bible inductively, but you apply their truths to where you're living today. The series of study books includes optional discussion questions for group leaders or to stimulate your own thinking, plus a thought for each week that challenges you to holiness.

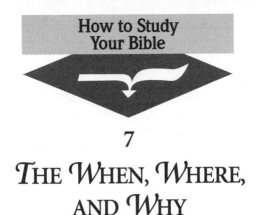

7

THE WHEN, WHERE, AND WHY

W hat was the occasion?" This is a phrase we commonly use when asking why something was done. "Occasion" is a word we need to use in studying the precious Word of God. (If it's ever taken away from us, we'll discover just how precious it is!)

Understanding the occasion of a book means we understand the circumstances that prompted its writing and the setting in which it was written. At times, this kind of understanding can be pivotal in interpreting the text properly. Anyone who has studied the book of Hebrews realizes this.

To discover the occasion and setting of a book, you need to do two things.

First, research the author's background.

- ∾ Do a character study from an inductive approach. For further information on this, see the section on "How to Do a Character Study."

- ∾ Read what commentaries have to say on the book you are studying. Usually they contain an introduction to the book in which they give pertinent information regarding the author, the setting and date of the book, and its structure. You will want to be careful, however, not to read any further in your commentaries than is absolutely necessary to identify the facts about the author. You do not want to spoil the joy of discovering truth for yourself!

∾ Read a book written by a credible scholar or teacher about the author of the book you are studying (e.g. a book about Paul). Become familiar with the biblical author's life and his works.

Second, examine the historical setting.

∾ The date of writing is usually discussed in commentaries in the introduction to the book. The *New Inductive Study Bible* records the date (if it's known) in the introduction to each book of the Bible.

∾ After you have observed all you can from the book itself regarding its historical setting, then look at Bible handbooks and Bible dictionaries. These can be of great help. Further insights on persons mentioned in a book can be gained by checking cross-references in your Bible and by using a concordance to find other related Scriptures. For example, if you want more information on Demas, who deserted Paul (2 Timothy 4:10), look up Demas in the concordance or in a topical Bible and you will find him mentioned in Colossians 4:14; 2 Timothy 4:10; and Philemon 1:24.

∾ The customs of the day shed great light on understanding exactly what God is saying, and many times will make the difference between correct and incorrect interpretation. Usually you'll do a study of the customs as you progress in your study of a book. There are a number of excellent books on biblical customs, and a few examples are included in the "Recommended Study Helps" at the end of this book. Commentaries may also provide further information on the customs of the day.

At this point are you thinking about how much time and work and effort it takes to truly delve into the Word and come to a right understanding of it? It takes a lot, Beloved. It is going to take some discipline on your part to do all this. And discipline is never easy.

But, O child of God, it's worth it. For all this is a matter of life—life on the highest plane!

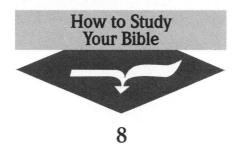

8

LET'S FIGURE IT OUT

∾∾∾∾∾

*P*eople can tell you God exists and that He knows and cares about you. But how do you know whether or not they are telling you the truth? After all, human beings can be wrong. So where can you find the truth about God—and be sure it is true? Only one place. In the one book that claims to be and has proven to be the Word of God. The Bible!

Although the Bible is the literal Word of God, inerrant in every aspect, it was written so that we human beings could understand it—it was written in the language of the people. It is a literary work, and literature is composed of various styles of writing, which in turn use a variety of figures of speech.

Therefore, when you seek to interpret the Word of God, you must handle the text properly, recognizing and respecting the figures of speech used in each book.

Discerning the use of figures of speech is important in biblical interpretation. For example, there has been much controversy in the church over Jesus' statement regarding the bread at the Last Supper:

> "When He had taken *some* bread *and* given thanks, He broke it and gave it to them, saying, 'This is My body which is given for you'" (Luke 22:19).

A figure of speech is a word, a phrase, or an expression used in a figurative rather than a literal sense.

Some believe that the bread actually becomes His body (the doctrine of transubstantiation); others believe that Jesus was simply using a *metaphor* and that the bread, therefore, is representative of His body. These differences occur because not all students of the Word adhere to the guidelines for interpreting figurative language.

Three Principles for Understanding Figurative Language

- ∾ Identify the fact that the author is using figurative language.

- ∾ Identify the type of figurative language in use: simile, metaphor, hyperbole, and so on.

- ∾ Follow the guidelines for interpreting what the author meant by his use of that particular figure of speech.

You will be aided in your study of Scripture if you are able to identify *when* the author is using a figure of speech. Following are brief definitions of the types of figurative language used in the Bible.

Simile

A *simile* is an expressed or stated comparison of two different things or ideas that uses the connecting words *like, as, such as* or the word pair *as...so.* For example:

"His eyes were like a flame of fire" (Revelation 1:14b).

"As the deer pants for the water brooks, so my soul pants for You, O God" (Psalm 42:1).

In these examples the use of *like* and *as...so* show you that these are stated comparisons or similes.

Metaphor

A *metaphor* is an implied comparison between two things that are different. A metaphor is different from a simile in that a metaphor is not a stated comparison; it is an implied comparison. In a metaphor the words of comparison *like, as,* and *such as* are **not** used. An example of three metaphors are found in John 15:5 and Ephesians 6:17.

In John 15:5 Jesus says, "I am the vine, you are the branches...." There are two metaphors in this verse. One compares Jesus with a vine, and the other compares His audience with branches. You have to study the context to discover who these people are.

Ephesians 6:17 says, "...the sword of the Spirit, which is the word of God." Here the Word of God is compared with a sword.

Exaggeration

Exaggeration, also called *hyperbole*, is a deliberate exaggeration for effect or emphasis. Hyperboles are found in all languages, however they are frequently used among Semitic peoples, and that's what the children of Israel were—Semitic people.

Psalm 119:20 says, "My soul is crushed with longing." Since a soul is an invisible thing, it cannot be literally crushed. But the use of the word "crushed" shows an exaggeration of grief.

In Matthew 23:24 it says, "You blind guides, who strain out a gnat and swallow a camel!" You see here the exaggeration of straining out a gnat and of swallowing a camel.

Metonymy

Metonymy is a figure of association, when the name of one object or concept is used for that of another to which it is related.

"All the country of Judea was going out to him" (Mark 1:5).

In this verse the metonymy is "country," which refers to the people rather than the region itself. Note also the hyperbole, "all the country."

Synecdoche

Synecdoche is another figure of association where the whole can refer to the part or the part to the whole.

> This is often found in the use of the term "the law," which can refer to the Pentateuch (the first five books of the Old Testament), the Ten Commandments, or the whole Old Testament.

A synecdoche can also be a singular for a plural or a plural for a singular.

> In Jeremiah 25:29 God says He is going to summon "a sword against all the inhabitants of the earth." The singular sword represents many swords.

Personification

In *personification* an object is given characteristics or attributes that belong to people.

> "The trees of the fields will clap their hands..." (Isaiah 55:12).

Irony

Irony is a statement which says the opposite of what is meant. Irony is used for emphasis or effect.

> In 1 Corinthians 4:8 Paul says to the Corinthians, "You are already filled, you have already become rich, you have become kings without us; and indeed, I wish that you had become kings so that we also might reign with you." It is obvious that the Corinthians are not kings, nor does Paul desire to reign with them; therefore, when you study this, you can determine that he is using irony to make a point.

> In 1 Kings 22:1-23, a true prophet tells the king what he wants to hear, but it is a lie. It's obvious he is using irony because the king tells him to stop prophesying falsely and to tell the truth.

When it is not easy to discern if a statement is ironic, then examine it first as a true statement. As such, does it make sense in its context? If not, examine it as irony. If this makes sense and fits with the context, then accept it as irony. Otherwise, treat it as a truth.

As you see, Beloved, all these figures of speech help us "figure out" what God is saying to us.

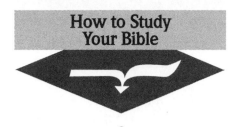

How to Study
Your Bible

9

WHEN ONE THING
REPRESENTS ANOTHER

If you listen long enough, you'll hear a wide variety of messages on and interpretations of the story of the prodigal son. But even though these presentations and insights may thrill an audience, one must ask, "Is the story being handled properly?" That's the question we must always ask. And to answer it, we must know how to deal with parables—one of several literary devices used often in the Scriptures.

If you're going to discern the true meaning of the text, then you need to be aware of parables, allegories, types, and symbols and how to handle them so you don't distort the author's purpose in using them.

Because these literary devices are so common and so significant to a right understanding of Scripture, they merit special attention, and thus they have their own section in this book. Let's look at each one.

Parables

A parable is a story that teaches a moral lesson or truth. Although it is not usually factual, a parable is a story that is true to life. It is designed to make one central point, and every detail of the parable will reinforce that main point. However, you should not always attempt to ascribe a specific spiritual meaning and application to each detail.

*Parables amplify or affirm doctrine
rather than establish it, because parables
are more obscure than clear doctrinal passages.*

Jesus frequently used parables in His teaching for two reasons:

∽ to reveal truth to believers, and

∽ to hide truth from those who had rejected it and/or hardened their hearts against it (Matthew 13:10-17; Mark 4:10-12).

To correctly interpret a parable:

STEP 1: *Determine the occasion of the parable.* Since parables clarify or emphasize a truth, search out the *Why* or *What* of the parable. *Why* was it told? *What* prompted it?

> Jesus told the parable of the prodigal son because He wanted the Pharisees to see what their hearts were like as they grumbled, "This man receives sinners and eats with them" (Luke 15:2).

> In the parable of the Pharisee and the tax collector in Luke 18:9, the *Why* is clear: "And He also told this parable to some people who trusted in themselves that they were righteous, and viewed others with contempt."

STEP 2: *Look for the explanation of the meaning of the parable.* This can be done by examining the context of the parable, specifically the interpretation of the parable that Jesus gave to the hearer(s).

Don't impose any meaning beyond what is clearly stated or applied to the hearers by the speaker of the parable.

STEP 3: *Identify the central or focal idea of the parable.* Every parable has one central theme or emphasis. No detail of the story is to be given any meaning that is independent of the main teaching of the parable.

For example, in the larger context surrounding the parable of the prodigal son, Jesus made His point by telling three consecutive parables about three things that were lost: a sheep, a coin, and a son. In each of the parables Jesus uses the following words: lost, found, sin, and joy (rejoice). When He tells the story of the prodigal son, He shows the kindness of the father's heart versus the hardness of the elder brother's heart. In doing so, He shows the Pharisees that their hearts are like the heart of the elder brother, not the heart of the father.

In the parable of the Pharisee and the publican in Luke 18, Jesus tells about the Pharisee and the tax gatherer going to the temple to pray. The main emphasis of the parable is given in verse 14: "...for everyone who exalts himself will be humbled, but he who humbles himself will be exalted."

STEP 4: *Since a parable has one central point of emphasis, you must identify the relevant details and the irrelevant details.*

A relevant detail will always reinforce the central point. Jesus demonstrates this basic rule of interpretation when He gives the parable of the sower and states, "Do you not understand this parable? How will you understand all the parables?" (Mark 4:13). From there Jesus proceeds to interpret the parable, identifying relevant details, all of which relate to one central emphasis: the reception of the Word of God by different people.

All details in a parable do not have significance, however. To attach a meaning that is not in the context or relevant to its central emphasis is to depart from the meaning of the parable. A detail is relevant only if it reinforces the central point of the parable.

STEP 5: *Interpret parables in the context of the culture of Bible times rather than the culture of today.*

For example, in the parable of the wise and foolish virgins, understanding Eastern wedding traditions gives insight into the parable and explains why some were ready and others were not. A book on the customs of Bible times or a good Bible dictionary can shed light on many of these traditions.

STEP 6: *Parables should never be the primary or only source for establishing doctrine.* Parables amplify or affirm doctrine rather than establish it, because parables are more obscure than clear doctrinal passages.

Allegory

An allegory is a story with an underlying meaning that differs from the surface facts of the story itself; in other words, it describes one thing by using the image of another. Some refer to an allegory as an extended metaphor (remember, a metaphor is an implied comparison between two different things). An allegory is a realistic or nonrealistic story created to teach one or more truths which may or may not be related.

Two examples that you can see in Scripture are the allegory of the vine and the branches in John 15:1-8 and the allegory of the bondwoman and the free woman presented in Galatians 4:21-31.

When interpreting an allegory, follow these guidelines:

STEP 1: *List the features of the allegory.* In Galatians 4:22-23 it states:

> "For it is written that Abraham had two sons, one by the bondwoman and one by the free woman. But the son by the bondwoman was born according to the flesh, and the son by the free woman through the promise."

STEP 2: *Note any interpretation given within the text of the allegory.*

The interpretation of Galatians 4:22-23 is found in verses 24-26,27-29,31:

> "This is allegorically speaking, for these women are two covenants: one *proceeding* from Mount Sinai bearing children who are to be slaves; she is Hagar. Now this Hagar is Mount Sinai in Arabia and corresponds to the present Jerusalem, for she is in slavery with her children. But the Jerusalem above is free; she is

our mother.... And <u>you brethren, like Isaac, are children of promise</u>. But as at that time he who was born according to the flesh persecuted him <u>who was born</u> according to the Spirit, so it is now also.... So then, <u>brethren, we are not children of a bondwoman, but of the free woman</u>."

STEP 3: *Do not contradict the clear teaching of the Word of God by interpreting an unexplained detail in an allegory in a way that would contradict clear teaching.* Study the allegory's features according to sound principles of biblical exegesis.

STEP 4: *Do not try to identify all the features of an allegory.*

For example, in the allegory of the vine and the branches in John 15, there is mention of people ("they" in verse 6) who gather the branches and throw them into the fire, but Jesus doesn't say who these people are.

The chart below comparing parables and allegories will help you distinguish one from the other.

COMPARING PARABLES AND ALLEGORIES

PARABLE	ALLEGORY
1. Has one central point.	1. Can have more than one central point.
2. Teaches one truth.	2. Can teach a number of truths.
3. Every relevant detail reinforces the central theme or point of emphasis.	3. The details of an allegory may be many and varied, relating to more than one theme.
4. Can have irrelevant details; all features of the parable do not have to be identified.	4. Can have irrelevant details; all features of an allegory do not have to be identified.
5. Usually the story is separate from its interpretation and application.	5. Intertwines the story and the meaning.
6. Interpretation usually follows the parable.	6. Interpretation is found within the allegory.

Types

A type is a prophetic symbol designated by God. The word "type" comes from the Greek word *tupos*. A tupos was a mark formed by a blow or an impression, creating a figure or an image on the object that was struck. Therefore, a type *prefigures* something or someone to come. That which it prefigures is called an antitype. A type prefigures only one antitype, although it may parallel many points in the antitype.

An example is found in Romans 5:14:

> "Nevertheless death reigned from Adam until Moses, even over those who had not sinned in the likeness of the offense of <u>Adam, who is a type of Him who was to come.</u>"

Adam is a type of Jesus, who is the antitype.

When determining types, although it may not be formally stated, there should be some evidence of divine affirmation of the corresponding type and antitype.

Remember, the example in Romans 5:14 clearly states that Adam was a type of Christ. In 1 Corinthians 15:45, Christ is referred to as "the last Adam." If the Word does not designate something as a type, then you should simply show the parallels without calling it a type.

Symbols

A symbol is a picture or an object that stands for or represents another thing. For example, the seven candlesticks mentioned in Revelation 1:20 represent the seven churches described in Revelation 2 and 3.

When noting symbols, remember the following:

1. The item used as a symbol can symbolize different things in different passages. For example, water is used to symbolize the Word of God (Ephesians 5:26) and the Holy Spirit (John 7:37-39).

2. Although a symbol can represent many things, when it does symbolize something in a given passage, a single parallel is intended.

For instance, in John 7:37-39 water symbolizes only the Holy Spirit, not the Word.

3. Interpret symbols in the light of the biblical setting and culture rather than the culture of the current interpreter.

4. Symbols are timeless and can symbolize something past, present, or future.

Well, my friend, you've learned much about the use of figures of speech. When you interpret the Word of God, interpret it literally, yet always remember that as you interpret it literally you must consider, appreciate, and correctly interpret the figures of speech used by the author.

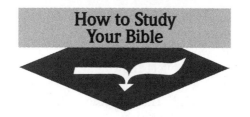
10

*U*NRAVELING *R*EVELATION

*T*he Bible shows us how to take what is wrong and make it right. Isn't that encouraging! It tells us how to live so that we can know how to handle every situation of life right now. But God doesn't stop there. He also tells us about the future.

From Genesis to Revelation, the Bible is filled with prophecy. The Greek word for prophecy, *propheteia*, comes from two Greek words: *pro*, meaning "forth," and *phemi*, meaning "to speak." Prophecy, therefore, means to speak forth the mind and counsel of God. Since in this sense all Scripture is prophecy, we will look only at the type of writing that is known as predictive prophecy.

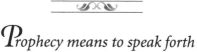

*P*rophecy means to speak forth
the mind and counsel of God.

Predictive prophecy points to a future fulfillment and is of divine origin. In *Understanding and Applying the Bible*, Dr. Robertson McQuilkin says:

"There are two purposes for predictive prophecy. The chief purpose is to affect the conduct of those who hear the prophecy. Another purpose is met only when the prophecy is fulfilled. That purpose is to establish confidence in the God who miraculously foretold events (John 13:19; 14:29; 16:4)."

Some scholars divide predictive prophecy into two categories: forthtelling and foretelling.

Forthtelling prophecies contain a message about the present or immediate time. Often this is a call to godly living in the light of prophecy yet to be fulfilled. In Daniel 4, God told King Nebuchadnezzar in a dream what would happen to him if he did not repent.

Foretelling prophecies contain a message about what God will do in the future. Daniel 7 lays out the course of history from Nebuchadnezzar's time through the second coming of the Lord Jesus Christ and the setting up of His kingdom on earth. Revelation 4–22 tells what God will do in the end times concerning judgment, Christ's coming, and the Bride of Christ.

When a prophet spoke for God, the prophecy could refer to the following:

∾ a present or near fulfillment

∾ a future fulfillment

∾ a twofold fulfillment: a near fulfillment and then a later, future fulfillment.

As you read the prophecies of the Bible, discern whether the prophecy refers to:

∾ the prophet's own time and/or a future time

∾ the captivity and/or restoration of Israel or Judah

∾ the first coming of Christ and any events connected with it

∾ the second coming of Christ

∾ the last days or end times.

Important Guidelines

If you want to handle the prophecies in the Word of God accurately, the following guidelines will give you some important parameters.*

PRINCIPLE 1: *The prophets did not always indicate intervals of time between events, nor did they always write their prophecies in chronological order.*

> For example, an Old Testament prophecy could include the first and second comings of Christ without any indication of the time span between the two comings.

One such prophecy is found in Isaiah 65:17-25. In this prophecy Isaiah first talks about the new heavens and the new earth, in which we know there is no death. Then in verses 18-25 he refers to a time when a youth will die at age 100 and the wolf and lamb will lie down together. Chronologically, however, verse 17 will be fulfilled after verses 18-25 become a reality.

PRINCIPLE 2: *Always approach a prophecy as literal (in its usual, ordinary sense of the words) unless one of the following occurs:*

A. The grammatical context shows that it is figurative language by the use of similes, metaphors, parables, allegories, symbols, or types.

> For example, consider Daniel 7, where four unusual beasts represent four kings and their kingdoms.

B. A literal interpretation violates common sense, is contrary to what the author is saying, or is contrary to what the rest of Scripture teaches.

> Again some examples can be seen in Daniel 7. One beast is described as a lion with the wings of an eagle, and another is described as a leopard with four wings and four heads. These descriptions violate common sense; therefore, there is no reason

---

* These are also listed in the Appendix of the *New Inductive Study Bible.*

to interpret these as literal; rather, they should be considered symbolic.

PRINCIPLE 3: *When a prophetic passage cannot be taken literally, look for what the author is trying to convey through his figurative or symbolic language.* To discern what the author is saying, look for answers in the following places:

A. Within the context of the book in which the passage appears.

In Daniel 7:17 it says, "These great beasts, which are four *in number*, are four kings *who* will arise from the earth."

B. In any other writings of that author or in other books which refer to the same person and/or event.

For example, the fourth beast in Daniel 7 parallels the beast in Revelation 13.

C. In any other prophetic writings to which the author had access.

For example, other prophetic books or passages in the Word of God. Revelation is filled with quotes from a number of Old Testament books.

PRINCIPLE 4: *Remember that often when a prophet refers to future events, he does not use the future tense.*

PRINCIPLE 5: *When you interpret Scripture, consider the historical context of that writing, remembering that God was delivering His prophecy to a particular people at a particular time.*

Granted, it might have been a prophecy with a future fulfillment, but it would still be delivered in a way that was comprehensible to those receiving that prophecy—although they might not understand the details, the symbolism, or the full implications of the prophecy.

For example, in Habakkuk God tells His people, Israel, that He is "raising up the Chaldeans" to judge Israel for their wickedness and violence (Habakkuk 1:6).

Make a careful historical and cultural analysis of the text. Determine the identity of all historical events, proper names, and geographical locations before you attempt to interpret the text.

PRINCIPLE 6: *Remember that the meaning of a specific prophecy could not always be understood by the prophet or by the people who heard the message* (1Peter 1:10-12).

For example, Daniel could not understand what he had written since it was to remain sealed until the end time (Daniel 12:8-9).

However, many prophecies will come to light through the following:

A. A fulfillment as recorded in history.

Daniel 11 is one of the most difficult chapters in the Bible. However, when combined with history, it becomes very easy to understand. Daniel 11:3 is a prophecy of Alexander the Great, and in verses 5-35 the "king of the North" refers to the Syrian kings from 312 B.C. to 163 B.C. and the "king of the South" refers to the Egyptian kings from 323 B.C. to 145 B.C. (There's a chart that fully explains this in the *New Inductive Study Bible*.)

B. A fulfillment as recorded in the New Testament.

In Matthew 1:22-23 it says, "Now all this took place to fulfill what was spoken by the Lord through the prophet: 'BEHOLD, THE VIRGIN SHALL BE WITH CHILD AND SHALL BEAR A SON, AND THEY SHALL CALL HIS NAME IMMANUEL,' which translated means, 'GOD WITH US.'" This tells of the fulfillment of Isaiah 7:14.

C. An explanation given by an Old Testament or a New Testament writing.

In Acts 4:24-28 Luke explains quotes from Exodus 20 and Psalm 2 as prophecies that were being fulfilled during the time of Jesus' trial and crucifixion.

PRINCIPLE 7: *Remember that many New Testament prophecies include Old Testament quotations and allusions.*

Scholars estimate that at least 350 Old Testament quotations or allusions appear in the book of Revelation alone. Revelation is replete with the language of Isaiah, Jeremiah, Ezekiel, Daniel, and the minor prophets. It is obvious that the author of Revelation was steeped in the Old Testament, for he talks in Old Testament phraseology.

So to correctly interpret New Testament prophecy, check Old Testament cross-references.

PRINCIPLE 8: *When you study prophecy, watch for phrases that indicate periods of time.* For example, look for "in the last days," "day of the Lord," "day of wrath," and "end of the age." When you come across phrases such as these, carefully observe the things which occur during that particular time period. Then ask the following questions:

A. Have these events ever occurred in history?

In Matthew 24:21,29-30 it says of a particular time, "for then there will be a great tribulation, <u>such as has not occurred since the beginning of the world until now, nor ever will.... But immediately after the tribulation of those days</u> THE SUN WILL BE DARKENED, AND THE MOON WILL NOT GIVE ITS LIGHT, AND THE STARS WILL FALL from the sky, and the powers of the heavens will be shaken. And then the sign of the Son of Man will appear in the sky, and then all the tribes of the earth will mourn, <u>and they will see the SON OF MAN COMING ON THE CLOUDS OF THE SKY with power and great glory.</u>"

The underlined portion tells us that there is a specific time immediately before Jesus comes again when there will be a great tribulation, greater than any since time began.

B. Do these events coincide with any other particular period of time?

You can see in the above example from Matthew 24 that the second coming of Jesus is connected with a time of great tribulation.

C. Do these events parallel any events mentioned in another place in the Word of God?

Again, in the example above we see that Matthew 24 presents another event that happens right before the time of the "great tribulation." It's the revelation of the "abomination of desolation."

Verse 15 says, "Therefore <u>when</u> you see the ABOMINATION OF DESOLATION which was spoken of through Daniel the prophet, standing in the holy place (let the reader understand)," and verse 21 continues with that time when it says, "for <u>then</u> there will be a great tribulation."

So you can see that one of the events of this time is the "abomination of desolation," and you can also see that it is spoken of in the book of Daniel. The next step would be to compare Daniel with Matthew.

Matthew 24 mentions a "great tribulation, such as has not occurred since the beginning of the world until now, nor ever will." This passage parallels Daniel 12:1: "And there will be a time of distress such as never occurred since there was a nation until that time."

Isn't it absolutely awesome the way God weaves His threads of truth throughout the Bible! So often when I study or write our Precept courses, I just have to stop and thank God for the beauty of His Word and the wonderful privilege of studying it!

The Bible is not some kind of crystal ball wherein we can see—or predict—what specific things God will bring to pass in each of our individual lives. But God does give us a glimpse of the "big picture" as He shows us what is in store for those who love Him.

So live your life accordingly, Beloved. Remember Jesus said, "I am coming quickly, and My reward is with Me, to render to every man according to what he has done" (Revelation 22:12).

❦

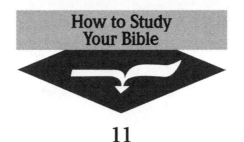

11

GETTING THE
POINT ACROSS

*T*he Bible was written to others and about others, but God tells us that what He wrote to others and about others is also for us and about us. The Bible is a timeless book—it's for all people for all time. And that means you, my friend. But to understand this timeless book, you must understand how it was written.

Laws of Composition

Good writing is the arrangement of thoughts in such a way as to clearly convey the author's intended meaning to a reader.

To describe the various ways authors arrange their thoughts, we use the term "laws of composition." Recognizing and understanding these "laws" will not only provide insight into the way language works, but will help you handle and interpret the Word of God.

Preparation or Introduction

The presentation of background information to prepare the reader for what follows is known as the *preparation* or *introduction.*

For example, the purpose of the Gospel of John is to prepare the reader to believe that Jesus is the Christ, the Son of God. In John 1:1-18 the writer thoroughly introduces his subject and prepares his readers for what is to come.

Comparison

Comparison is the comparing of things in order to show similarities. A comparison is the association of like things.

> An example is found in 2 Timothy 2:3: "Suffer hardship with me, as a good soldier of Christ Jesus."

Contrast

A *contrast* compares things in order to show differences. Contrast is the association of opposites.

> An example is found in 2 Timothy 1:9: "who has saved us and called us with a holy calling, not according to our works, but according to His own purpose and grace...."

> This contrast is telling believers how we were saved and called; God did it all, not us. It is according to His purpose and grace and not our works.

Repetition

Repetition is using the same word or phrase a number of times.

> In John 1:1-14, "the Word" is repeated four times.

Progression

Progression is an extension of a specific theme throughout a portion of Scripture. Many times the author will amplify what he is saying or add to what he has said as he progresses in his writing.

> In John 1:1-17 certain details are revealed about "the Word," such as the facts that He was in the beginning, was with God,

was God, created all things, in Him was life, and He became flesh. Then in verse 14 you are told that He is full of grace and truth: "And the Word became flesh, and dwelt among us, and we saw His glory, glory as of the only begotten from the Father, full of grace and truth." Verse 17 then reveals that the author had been speaking of Jesus: "For the Law was given through Moses; grace and truth were realized through Jesus Christ."

Climax

A *climax* is the high point built by a progression from the lesser to the greater. A climax is simply the extension of the law of progression until it reaches a peak of intensity.

In the illustration just noted from John 1:1-17, you can see the facts revealing things about "the Word," but "the Word" is not identified completely until verse 17. The climax of this description of God who became flesh is reached when you are told that He is Jesus Christ.

Pivotal Point

A *pivotal point* is a changing or a turning in which the elements on each side of the point differ in some way.

The pivotal point in the Gospel of John comes in 11:54 when Jesus turns from ministering mainly to the public to ministering to His disciples: "Therefore Jesus no longer continued to walk publicly among the Jews, but went away from there to the country near the wilderness, into a city called Ephraim; and there He stayed with the disciples."

The pivotal point of the book of Genesis comes in chapter 12, where Moses turns from recording major events to tell us of major characters.

Radiation

Radiation is the central or single point from which or to which other truths point.

An illustration of this is found in 1 Corinthians 15, where the truths of that chapter all radiate to resurrection.

Interchange

Interchange is the alternating, in sequence, of at least two main thoughts, subjects, or characteristics.

This is most apparent in the Gospel of Luke. Luke opens with the announcement of the birth of John the Baptist, then moves to the announcement of Jesus' birth. He then returns to John the Baptist's birth, then to the birth of Christ. This is alternation or interchange.

General to Particular

General to particular (or vice versa) is a move from the extensive or general to the specific.

This is beautifully seen in Genesis 1 and 2. Genesis 1 gives the general overview of creation, including the creation of mankind, male and female, on the sixth day. Genesis 2 moves from the general to the particular, giving more details of the creation of man and of woman.

Cause and Effect

Cause and effect (or vice versa) is a move from the source to the consequence.

An example of this is found in John 11. Verse 4 states that the cause of the death of Lazarus, the beloved friend of Christ, was to glorify the Son:

> "But when Jesus heard this, He said, 'This sickness is not to end in death, but for the glory of God, so that the Son of God may be glorified by it.'"

The effect is seen in verse 45 where the people believed on Christ after seeing His power in raising Lazarus:

"Therefore many of the Jews who came to Mary, and saw what He had done, believed in Him."

The effect is also seen in John 12:17-18, where again the Son is glorified:

"So the people who were with Him when He called Lazarus out of the tomb and raised him from the dead continued to testify about Him. For this reason also the people went and met Him, because they heard that He had performed this sign."

Explanation or Analysis

Explanation or *analysis* is the presentation of an idea or event followed by its explanation.

This is expertly done by our Lord in John 6, where He multiplies the loaves and the fishes and then says that He is the bread who gives us life.

Interrogation

Interrogation is the presentation of a question, usually followed by its answer.

Paul uses this technique to full advantage in writing Romans. Paul anticipates his readers' questions or objections, states them usually as a question, and then proceeds to answer the very questions he has raised.

Romans 6 demonstrates this technique: "What shall we say then? Are we to continue in sin so that grace may increase? May it never be!" (verses 1-2).

Summarization

Summarization is restating the main points, to sum up or to briefly restate particular truths.

Moses does this in Deuteronomy 1–4 as he rehearses before the children of Israel those things that took place following the exodus from Egypt.

And in Acts 7 Stephen provides a masterful summarization of Israel's history.

Now, I know all this is a lot to digest. But just think about how it can impact your understanding of the Word of God!

∽∾∿∽∿∾∽

Part Three

APPLICATION

Discover How It Works!

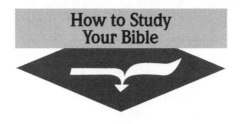
12

THE TRANSFORMED LIFE

∽∽∽∽∽∽

*B*ible study is much more than an intellectual classroom exercise, of course. It is a life-transforming process. Thus, we come to the very critical part of the inductive process—application. Once you know what a passage means, you are responsible to live it.

Application flows out of thorough observation and correct interpretation. Application begins with belief, which then results in doing. It takes place as you are confronted with the truth and respond to it in obedience, and the glorious end result is transformation. You're made more like your Lord and Savior, Jesus Christ.

No matter how much you know about God's Word, if you don't apply what you learn, Scripture will never benefit your life. To be a hearer of the Word and not a doer is to deceive yourself (James 1:22-25). This is why application is so vital. Observation and interpretation are the "hearing" of God's Word. Application is the embracing of the truth, the "doing" of God's Word.

Application answers the questions:

∽ *How* does the meaning of this passage apply to me?

∽ *What* truths am I to embrace, believe, or order my life by?

∽ *What* changes should I make in my belief, in my life?

Second Timothy 3:16-17 gives us the *How* of application. Listen:

"All Scripture is inspired by God and profitable for teaching, for reproof, for correction, for training in righteousness; so that the man of God may be adequate, equipped for every good work."

Thus, we must apply Scripture in the light of its *teaching, reproof, correction,* and *training in righteousness.* This is the key to application—the key to its instructions for our life.

No matter how much you know about God's Word,
if you don't apply what you learn,
Scripture will never benefit your life.

Teaching (doctrine) is what the Word of God says on any particular subject. That teaching is always true. Therefore, everything that God says in His Word about any given subject is absolute truth.

STEP 1: The first step in the application of truth is to find out what the Word of God says on any particular subject through accurate observation and correct interpretation of the text.

STEP 2: Then, once you understand what the Word of God teaches, you are obligated before God to accept that truth and to live by it.

STEP 3: When you have adjusted any false concepts or teaching you may have believed and have embraced the truth revealed in God's Word, then you have applied what you have learned.

Reproof exposes areas in your thinking and behavior that do not align with God's Word. Reproof is finding out where you have thought wrongly or where you haven't been doing what God says is right.

The application of reproof is to accept it and agree with God, acknowledging where you are wrong in thought or in behavior. This is how you are set free from unbelief and from sin.

Correction is the next area of application, and often the most difficult. Many times you can see what is wrong, but perhaps you are reluctant to take the necessary steps to correct it.

God has not left you without help or without answers in this step of correcting what is wrong. Sometimes the answers are difficult to find, but they are always there, and any child of God who wants to please his or her Father will be shown by the Spirit of God how to do so. Many times correction comes by simply confessing and forsaking what is wrong. Other times, God gives very definite steps to take.

When you apply correction to your actions and attitudes, God will work in you to do His good pleasure (Philippians 2:13). Joy will follow obedience.

Training in righteousness: Although God's Word is profitable for reproof and correction, the Bible was also given to you as a handbook for living. As you spend time studying His Word, God equips you through:

- ◌ teachings
- ◌ commands
- ◌ promises
- ◌ exhortations
- ◌ warnings
- ◌ the lives of biblical characters
- ◌ accounts of God's dealings with man.

As you get into the Word of God and get to know God, you see how God intends for you to live. To live the way God says to live is to live righteously.

Scripture has everything you need to meet any and all situations of life, so that you "may be adequate, equipped for every good work" (2 Timothy 3:17). This, friend, is why you must study to show yourself approved unto God.

The Bible is your textbook for life. Don't fail your exam!

In other words, don't neglect the process of application. But remember: Application must be based on correct observation and accurate interpretation of the Word of God. Otherwise, you'll slip into legalism, or tradition that overrides truth, or some aberrant lifestyle that has an air of religion but is contrary to a correct relationship with God. The most effective application takes place as you go before the Lord and talk with Him about those things you have read, seen, heard, and carefully studied.

In applying Scripture to your life, the following questions may be helpful.

1. What does the passage teach?

   ∾ Is it general or specific?

   ∾ Does it apply only to specific people? To a cultural problem of the day? To a certain time in history?

   ∾ Has it been superseded by a broader teaching?

   For example, in the Old Testament the children of Israel were not allowed to eat certain foods. This prohibition is not applicable to Christians today because it was superseded by the teaching in Acts 10 and the account of Peter and his vision of the unclean animals.

2. Does this section of Scripture expose any error in your beliefs or in your behavior?

   ∾ Are there any commandments that you have not obeyed?

   ∾ Are there any wrong attitudes or motives in your life that the Scriptures bring to light?

3. What is God's instruction to you as His child?

   ∾ Are there any new truths to be believed?

   ∾ Are there any new commandments to be acted upon?

   ∾ Are there any new insights you are to pursue?

   ∾ Are there any promises you are to embrace?

When applying Scripture, beware of the following:

1. Applying cultural standards rather than biblical standards.

2. Attempting to strengthen a legitimate truth by using a Scripture incorrectly.

3. Applying Scripture out of prejudice from past training or teaching.

And don't forget that observation, interpretation, and application lead to *transformation.*

Ultimately the goal of personal Bible study is a transformed life and a deep and abiding relationship with Jesus Christ. Through it you are changed from glory to glory into the image of Jesus. Go for it!

Part Four

ORGANIZATION

Broaden Your Skills!

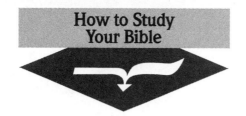

13

OUTLINING — JUST THE BARE FACTS

Sometimes your study might involve analyses of long passages of the Bible. To save time and much writing, you could outline the material, rather than writing out your information in the form of a composition. Outlining is an easy, concise way to visually identify the main points and logical flow of a book or passage of Scripture.

The purpose of an outline is to show in "skeletal" form the progression of the main or principal ideas of a book or subject. It is the organization of material in a logical form, without all the details. Like a skeleton, an outline is the bare bones without all the flesh.

General Principles of Outlining

Details may vary, but the form of an outline follows these general principles:

Principle 1: Main topics are the central ideas.

These should be briefly and clearly stated and should not be too numerous. If you are outlining a book of the Bible, these would probably be the chapter themes (summary statement of the main theme of a chapter) or segment divisions. If you are outlining a chapter, these might be the paragraph themes. They are denoted on an outline by Roman numerals: I, II, III, etc.

Principle 2: Subtopics are the points that explain the main topics.

In an outline of a book, these would be the paragraph themes. They are denoted by capital letters: A, B, C, etc.

Principle 3: Subpoints are the points that explain the subtopic.

These are denoted by Arabic numerals: 1, 2, 3, etc. If further subdivisions are necessary, they should be noted in progression as

   a.

     1)

       a)

        (1)

          (a)

Notice how the numbers and letters follow through and how the indentation occurs as each level of detail is added.

Principle 4: Capture the logical flow of the author.

To be sure that your outline truly captures the logical flow of the author, the subdivisions should do at least one or more of the following:

- ∾ Clarify or explain the main point of the previous larger subdivision.

- ∾ Classify points of the larger subdivision into categories.

- ∾ Define what the larger subdivision means.

- ∾ Serve as examples of the larger subdivision.

∾ List further details of the larger subdivision.

∾ Illustrate the larger subdivision.

Principle 5: Each subdivision must have at least two points.

If there is a Roman numeral I, there has to be at least a Roman numeral II. If there is an A, there must be a B. There can be more (C, D, etc.), but there have to be at least two points under each subdivision or it shouldn't be included.

Now let me give you an example of all this. Remember I said examples help me "see" what I've read?

TITLE

I. Main Topic
   A. Subtopic
   B. Subtopic
      1. subpoint
      2. subpoint
II. Main Topic
   A. Subtopic
      1. subpoint
         a. subpoint
         b. subpoint
            1) subpoint
            2) subpoint
               a) subpoint
               b) subpoint
                  (1) subpoint
                  (2) subpoint
                     (a) subpoint
                     (b) subpoint
      2. subpoint
   B. Subtopic

Now that you know "the way" to outline, let us give you two sample outlines from 2 Timothy. The first is a short, succinct outline of the whole book of 2 Timothy. The second is a very detailed outline of 2 Timothy 1, which we'll walk you through step by step.

As you look at these outlines, just realize that when *you* study 2 Timothy, or any book, inductively, you'll be able to come up with outlines similar to these. They are the harvest of your study!

Short Outline of 2 Timothy

GUARD THE TREASURE ENTRUSTED TO YOU

I. Retain the standard of sound words (chapter 1)

   A. Paul to Timothy (1:1-2)

   B. Do not be ashamed (1:3-14)

   C. Onesiphorus was not ashamed (1:15-18)

II. Entrust to faithful men (chapter 2)

   A. Remember Jesus Christ according to my gospel (2:1-13)

   B. Be diligent to be approved unto God/accurately handle the Word (2:14-26)

III. Continue in the things learned (chapter 3)

IV. Preach the Word (chapter 4)

   A. Fulfill your ministry (4:1-8)

   B. Be on guard against Alexander (4:9-18)

   C. Come before winter (4:19-21)

   D. Grace be with you (4:22)

Detailed Outline of 2 Timothy 1

First, since this is an outline of chapter 1, we will let the summary statement or the main theme of the chapter serve as the title of the outline:

RETAIN THE STANDARD OF SOUND WORDS

Now you need to determine the main topics of the chapter. The chapter can be divided into three paragraphs, each one discussing a main topic. Therefore, the paragraph themes serve as your three main topics.

RETAIN THE STANDARD OF SOUND WORDS

I. Paul greets Timothy (vv. 1-2)

II. Paul instructs Timothy to not be ashamed of the gospel (vv. 3-14)

III. Paul gives Onesiphorus as an example (vv. 15-18)

Then you can turn to each of the main topics (in this case paragraphs) and look at the subtopics and subpoints about each of these main topics, seeing how they clarify or explain the main point, classify points of the larger subdivision, define what the larger subdivision means, serve as examples of the larger subdivision, list further details of the larger subdivision, or illustrate the larger subdivision.

RETAIN THE STANDARD OF SOUND WORDS

I. Paul greets Timothy (vv. 1-2)

    A. as an apostle of Christ Jesus (v. 1)

    B. as a son whom he loves (v. 2)

    C. wishing him grace, mercy, and peace (v. 2)

Here you can see that these three subtopics give further details of how Paul greets Timothy. If you look at Paul's statement of greeting as an apostle, you can see two details of his apostleship for which you might create another level of subdivision (subpoints). And if you look at Paul's wish for Timothy to have grace, mercy, and peace, you can see that these have two sources, giving further details of this point. So your outline of the first paragraph would look like this:

RETAIN THE STANDARD OF SOUND WORDS

I. Paul greets Timothy (vv. 1-2)

    A. as an apostle of Christ Jesus (v. 1)

        1. by the will of God (v. 1)

        2. according to the promise of life in Christ Jesus (v. 1)

    B. as a son whom he loves (v. 2)

    C. wishing him grace, mercy, and peace (v. 2)

        1. from God the Father (v. 2)

        2. from Christ Jesus our Lord (v. 2)

Observe the indentation at each new level and that under each level there are at least two topics or subtopics.

Now, turn to the second main point, which is the heart of how Paul tells Timothy to "Retain the Standard of Sound Words." Paul tells Timothy that he must not be ashamed of the gospel and how and why he shouldn't.

II. Paul instructs Timothy to not be ashamed of the gospel (vv. 3-14)

At this point you need to examine the Scripture text to discover the subtopics under this second main topic and ensure that you have more than one subtopic, i.e., A, B, etc. In verses 3-7, Paul exhorts Timothy by telling him how much he has been blessed by Timothy and how Timothy has been blessed by God. In verse 8, you see the subpoint of instruction about not being ashamed, but joining in suffering for the gospel; in verses 9-10 you see reminders of what God has done through the gospel; in verses 11-12, Paul gives his own example; and in verses

13-14 he gives Timothy two more commands. Look at how this might serve as the basis for subtopics.

   II. Paul instructs Timothy to not be ashamed of the gospel (vv. 3-14)

      A. Paul thanks God for Timothy (vv. 3-4)

      B. Paul serves God (v. 3)

      C. Paul is mindful of Timothy's faith (v. 5)

      D. Paul reminds Timothy about his gift (v. 6)

      E. Paul recalls what God has given (v. 7)

      F. Paul commands Timothy to join him (vv. 8-11)

      G. Paul gives his own example (v. 12)

Now, if you want an even more comprehensive outline, for each of these subtopics, you would explore the subpoints that the Scripture gives you.

At this point, the temptation is to use your own words to paraphrase, but the greatest value will be derived from using the actual words of Scripture. Why? Because all this helps you remember what the text says. Every word of God is pure (Psalm 12:6). Therefore, the very process of doing it this way helps you "to retain the standard of sound words."

This is what the outline would look like with additional subpoints.

RETAIN THE STANDARD OF SOUND WORDS

   I. Paul greets Timothy (vv. 1-2)

      A. as an apostle of Christ Jesus (v. 1)

         1. by the will of God (v. 1)

         2. according to the promise of life in Christ Jesus (v. 1)

      B. as a son whom he loves (v. 2)

      C. wishing him grace, mercy, and peace (v. 2)

         1. from God the Father (v. 2)

         2. from Christ Jesus our Lord (v. 2)

II. Paul instructs Timothy to not be ashamed of the gospel (vv. 3-14)

    A. Paul thanks God for Timothy (vv. 3-4)

        1. as he constantly remembers him in prayer (v. 3)

        2. longing to see him (v. 4)

        3. seeing him would fill him with joy (v. 4)

    B. Paul serves God (v. 3)

        1. with a clear conscience (v. 3)

        2. the way his forefathers did (v. 3)

    C. Paul is mindful of Timothy's faith (v. 5)

        1. that first dwelt in his grandmother and mother (v. 5)

        2. that Paul is sure is in Timothy (v. 5)

    D. Paul reminds Timothy to kindle afresh his gift (v. 6)

    E. Paul recalls what God has given (v. 7)

        1. that God has not given a spirit of timidity (v. 7)

        2. that God has given a spirit of power, love, and discipline (v. 7)

When you get to this subtopic, it's probably easier to go ahead and explore all the subpoints and finish this subtopic before moving on to the other subtopics. This example of subtopic F shows the kind of detail you could go into, depending on your intent and interest.

    F. Paul commands Timothy to join him in suffering (vv. 8-11)

        1. for the gospel (as a result of not being ashamed of the gospel) (v. 8)

        2. according to the power of God (v. 8)

        3. because of God (vv. 9-10)

            a. who saved us (v. 9)

            b. and called us (v. 9)

1) with a holy calling (v. 9)

2) not according to our works (v. 9)

3) but according to His own purpose and grace (v. 9)

    a) granted us (v. 9)

        (1) in Christ Jesus (v. 9)

        (2) from all eternity (v. 9)

    b) but now revealed by the appearing of our Savior Christ Jesus (v. 10)

4. because of the gospel (vv. 10-12)

    a. through it (v. 10)

        1) death abolished (v. 10)

        2) life and immortality brought to light (v. 10)

    b. for it (v. 11)

        1) Paul appointed a preacher, apostle, and teacher (v. 11)

        2) Paul suffers unashamedly (v. 12)

G. Paul gives his own example (v. 12)

    1. suffers but is not ashamed (v. 12)

    2. knows whom he has believed (v. 12)

    3. is convinced He is able to guard what has been entrusted to Him (v. 12)

And finally, the third major topic, Onesiphorus, has several subtopics and few subpoints.

III. Paul gives Onesiphorus as an example (vv. 15-18)

    A. not like all in Asia, including Phygelus and Hermogenes, who turned away from Paul (v. 15)

    B. who often refreshed Paul (v. 16)

C. who was not ashamed of Paul's chains (v. 16)

D. who when in Rome (v. 16)

    1. eagerly searched for Paul (v. 17)

    2. found Paul (v. 17)

E. who rendered services in Ephesus (v. 18)

Because of the length of the passage examined in this example, we were able to show the extent of the detail that can be incorporated in an outline. With only one chapter, every important point can be included to see the logical flow of thought.

With a longer passage—for example an entire book—you would give less detail so that you can clearly see the most important points of the author's organization of the book.

The key is to remember that the Scripture itself gives you the words for the outline, showing you what the author has said. Therefore, there is no need for you to be "creative" and impose on Scripture what the Scripture doesn't say.

Well, those are the bare facts—but think of the insight and study they represent. When you do something like this, you'll know the vital facts of the book you've studied!

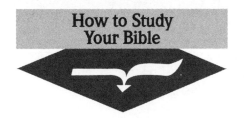

14

STUDYING TOPICALLY
BY SUBJECT

~~~~~~

A topical study is a comprehensive and exhaustive study of what God's Word has to say regarding a specific topic. It is much like a word study, only far more comprehensive. The advantage of a topical study is that it gives the total picture of what the Word of God has to say on a particular subject.

Topical studies, if done properly, require an enormous amount of preparation and a commitment to the integrity of accurately handling the Word. Following are four principles to use as guidelines for doing a topical study.

~~~~~

PRINCIPLE ONE

Look Up Every Parallel and Relative Passage on the Subject

When the same subject or account is mentioned in two or more books of the Bible, these passages are known as *relative* or *parallel passages.*

129

It's essential that you search out every related passage, understand and analyze it within its context, and then faithfully integrate it with all the other material you gather in your study.

A topical study gives the total picture of what the Word of God has to say on a particular subject.

To do this, you must begin by collecting your data!

∾ Use a concordance, a topical Bible (i.e. *Nave's*), or the chain-reference system in your Bible to find all the references to the subject you are studying. (If you use the chain-reference system in your Bible, remember that it will not be comprehensive.)

∾ Look up all related words. For example, if you are studying prayer, then also check "ask," "intercession," "supplication," "cried," and "petition."

∾ Look for the major topical passage that covers the subject in the most comprehensive way and for the passage where the subject is first mentioned in the Bible. Study these thoroughly.

∾ Look up any contrasting passages.

For example, if you were to do a topical study on the sovereignty of God, you should consider those passages that deal with the responsibility and accountability of man.

Considering contrasting passages helps you stay balanced in your theology and keeps you from going overboard in any one direction.

PRINCIPLE *T*WO

Assemble Your Information

Look up each reference on your list. If it is pertinent to your study, then as you study each related passage, note key verses along with the truths you have gleaned from them.

- ⌒ Study the passage thoroughly, examining it to ascertain the author's intended meaning.

- ⌒ Check the context carefully.

- ⌒ Determine the main truths taught in the passage.

- ⌒ Record your observations and new insights.

- ⌒ Note which passages are clear and which seem obscure. (An obscure passage is one with an unclear meaning.) *Do not build doctrine on passages that are unclear or obscure!*

- ⌒ Note how often a particular teaching is repeated. If it's repeated, give it greater attention. Make sure you put the emphasis where God puts the emphasis!

PRINCIPLE *T*HREE

Organize Your Material into an Outline

For help in outlining, see chapter 13, "Outlining—Just the Bare Facts."

- ⌒ Make sure you have a coherent and complete coverage of the topic.

- ⌒ Never build doctrine on inference, tradition, or extra-biblical sources. The Bible covers the subject as adequately and as thoroughly as is needed.

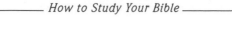

PRINCIPLE *F*OUR

Pray and Meditate on the Truth

God has revealed truths to you through His Word. Ask God to show you how to put into practice in your life what His Word says.

You know, Beloved, if we'd do more thorough topical studies like this, we'd have less controversy among believers. For instance, think of all the controversy that has come over the "baptism of the Spirit." If only people would study this subject and not add their experiences to what the Bible says, but let the Bible speak for itself, it would make a world of difference and heal many schisms.

Yet how many people do you know who are serious about obeying 2 Timothy 2:15 and studying so they handle God's Word accurately? Shame on us for so entangling ourselves in the affairs of this life that we forget what God has called us to.

∽∾∾∽

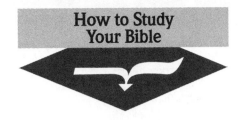
15

CHARACTER STUDIES—LEARNING FROM THE LIVES OF OTHERS

*hroughout His Word, God has given us true stories of people who have experienced victories, defeats, second chances, struggles, ecstasies, and depressions—people just like us.

When you study God's interactions with these men and women, both when they were doing well and when they were not, you can gain a better realization of God's holiness, sovereignty, longsuffering, and righteous ways. As you observe how He dealt with people in the Bible, you can see patterns for His dealings with people today. That's why character studies are valuable.

After you decide on the character you want to study, follow these guidelines.

STEP ONE

Gather All the Information on the Character

List every mention of that character in the Bible.

To find the passages where the character is mentioned, use one or more of the following study helps:

- an exhaustive concordance

- *Nave's Topical Bible*

- the cross-reference system in your Bible

STEP TWO

Read and Make Notes of Main Truths

As you do, remember the importance of context. Look for things like the following:

- *Meaning of name*—in Scripture, the meaning of a person's name is sometimes significant.

    For example, *Moses* means "to draw out of water."

    Caution: A person's name is not always significant, nor can its meaning always be used to determine his or her character.

- *Ancestry*—who were the character's father, mother, tribe, nation?

    For example, Moses was born an Israelite, but raised an Egyptian. This gave him a unique perspective and also created considerable difficulties for him.

- *Training and conversion*—what caused the character to turn toward God, or to turn away from Him? What was this person's upbringing like, where did it occur? Ask the 5 W's and an H about his/her life.

- *Times lived in, number of years lived, periods of life.*

For example, Moses' life is divided into three significant 40-year periods.

∾ *Shortcomings and accomplishments.*

∾ *Spiritual life*—what about the character's prayer life, obedience, suffering, personal lessons learned from God, attitudes, responses, reactions?

∾ *Scriptures that can be used as cross-references to illustrate spiritual principles*—discovering these references will become easier through regular inductive study of the many books of the Bible.*

For example, God does not show partiality in dealing with His leaders. He is to be obeyed, to be "sought the proper way." When Moses smote the rock a second time, God disciplined him (Numbers 20:2-12). Compare this with David moving the ark of the covenant (1 Samuel 6:1-8; 1 Chronicles 13:1-14; 15:1-3).

∾ *Effect of his/her life on others.*

∾ *The way he/she died and the impact of his/her death.*

STEP THREE

Check Out Extra-biblical References

After you have gleaned everything you can on your own from the Word of God, read a good Bible dictionary or other reference books to see what they have to say about the person you are studying. This can help to reinforce what you have learned. However, as you check out these references, make sure you bring them to the plumb line of God's Word.

---

* The International Inductive Study Series (Harvest House Publishers) will be most helpful.

STEP *F*OUR

Compile Your Material

Once you've completed your research, organizing the truths you have discovered can be done several different ways, depending on the emphasis you choose to make. You could organize it:

- ∿ Chronologically from birth to death.

- ∿ According to major events in the person's life.

  For example, the events in Moses' life can be divided into three 40-year periods: in Egypt, "on the back side of the desert," and leading the children of Israel.

- ∿ According to principles of life or ministry.

  Example: Moses the intercessor, Moses the leader.

STEP *F*IVE

Apply Truth to Your Own Life

Finally, after all this study, don't fail to apply the truths you have discovered to your own life.

Using the first person (I, me, my) list or write out in some detail the major truths God has taught you. For example:

- I know that to be used of God I must be taught of God as Moses was.

- I might be in a hurry to do God's work, as was Moses (Acts 7:23-35), but God is not in a hurry. First, He must equip and prepare me until I see that only God can do God's work.

- "God, reveal this truth to me in all its fullness."

When I think of character studies, I think of Paul's words in 1 Corinthians 11:1: "Be imitators of me, just as I also am of Christ." That's what I want to be—like Jesus. Isn't that what you want also, my friend? Of course it is. Then let's spend time sitting at His feet in His Word. It's the one thing that is needful. The one thing that can never be taken away (Luke 10:38-42).

Part Five

PRACTICAL HELPS

Tools for Further Study

APPENDIX A

Summary of the Inductive Process

⚬⚬⚬⚬⚬

Step One: *Overview*

1. Begin and continue with an attitude of prayer.

2. Read and re-read the book to be studied.

3. Identify the type of literature with which you are dealing.

4. Deal with the book objectively.

5. As you continually read, be sure that you are reading with a purpose by asking the 5 W's and an H (who, what, when, where, why, and how) kinds of questions.

6. To discover the context of any book, begin by identifying the facts about any people and events mentioned.

7. Read and re-read the text until you discover those words and phrases that are repeated. Mark these key words and phrases. Then make brief lists in the margin of the text from the key words and phrases.

8. Identify the main theme that best summarizes the book (the summary statement).

9. Construct an "At a Glance Chart."

10. Discover a theme (summary statement) for each chapter which both supports the book theme and encompasses the theme or message in each chapter.

11. Identify segment divisions.

Step Two: *Chapter Study*

1. Begin with prayer.

2. Read through the Observation Worksheet of the chapter looking for those things that are obvious.

3. Deal with the chapter objectively.

4. Read with a purpose by asking 5 W's and an H (who, what, when, where, why, and how) kinds of questions.

5. Look for the obvious.

6. Look for and mark key words and/or key phrases.

7. Make lists from the key words.

8. God reveals truth in many ways in His Word. Read through the text again looking for each of the following: contrasts, comparisons, terms of conclusion, and expressions of time.

9. Determine the chapter theme (summary statement).

10. Determine the paragraph themes (summary statements).

Step Three: *Word Studies*

1. The purpose for doing word studies is to understand the meaning of a word or words in the context you are studying.

2. The essential word study tools are an exhaustive concordance and an expository dictionary of biblical words.

3. Further word study skills—discovering the meaning of the original Greek or Hebrew words—can be helpful to a correct interpretation and application of Scripture.

Step Four: *Cross-References*

1. A cross-reference is a reference to another Scripture that supports, illumines, or amplifies the Scripture you are studying.

2. The best interpretation of Scripture is other Scripture.

3. Helpful tools are a concordance, a topical Bible, or the reference system in your own Bible.

At a Glance Chart

〜〜〜〜〜〜

JOHN AT A GLANCE

Theme of John: Eternal life through Jesus Christ, Son of God

SEGMENT DIVISIONS

Structure of Book	Written	Signs and Miracles	Ministry	#	CHAPTER THEMES
Introduces Jesus as Christ, Son of God	That you may believe Jesus is the Christ, Son of God	Water to wine	To Israel	1	Prologue – The Word / John the Baptist / calling disciples
				2	wedding Cana / cleansing temple
Gives signs that prove Jesus is Christ, Son of God		Heals noble man's son		3	born again
		Heals lame man		4	woman at well / royal official
		Feeds 5,000		5	father / son
		Walks on water		6	bread / feeding 5,000
				7	feast of tabernacles / thirst-drink
		Heals blind man		8	adulterous woman / truth sets free
		Raises Lazarus from dead		9	blind man
				10	sheep / shepherd
				11	raising Lazarus
Decision time	Life that belongs to those who believe God	Hour has come	To Disciples	12	dinner at Bethany / King on donkey
				13	last supper / washing-disciples
				14	Father's house / hearts be troubled
				15	abide / vine and branches
				16	Holy Spirit / another helper
				17	Lord's prayer / high-priestly prayer
Obtaining of that life – by death and resurrection	That you may have life		To All Mankind	18	arrest and trial
				19	crucifixion
		Resurrection appearances		20	resurrection
Purpose of life: love and follow			To Disciples	21	do you love Me?

Author: John

Date: about A.D. 85

Purpose: that his readers would believe that Jesus is the Christ, God's Son, and thus have eternal life

Key Words: (including synonyms)
signs / miracles
believe
life
judge
judgment
witness
sin
true, truth
king
kingdom
love
works
commandments
fruit
abide
ask
truth, truly, true
devil (Satan, ruler of this world)

Observation Worksheet *
2 Timothy
Chapter One

Chapter 1 Theme _Retain the Standard_

Paul to Timothy

1 Paul, ᵃan apostle of ᵇChrist Jesus ¹ᶜby the will of God, according to the promise of ᵈlife in Christ Jesus,

2 To Timothy, my beloved ¹ᵇson: ᶜGrace, mercy *and* peace from God the Father and Christ Jesus our Lord.

Do not be ashamed

3 ᵃI thank God, whom I ᵇserve with a ᶜclear conscience ¹the way my forefathers did, ᵈas I constantly remember you in my ²prayers night and day,

4 ᵃlonging to see you, ᵇeven as I recall your tears, so that I may be filled with joy.

5 ¹For I am mindful of the ᵃsincere faith within you, which first dwelt in your grandmother Lois and ᵇyour mother Eunice, and I am sure that *it is* in you as well.

6 For this reason I remind you to kindle afresh ᵃthe gift of God which is in you through ᵃthe laying on of my hands.

7 For God has not given us a ᵃspirit of ¹timidity, but of ⓵power and ⓶love and ²discipline. ⓷

8 Therefore ᵃdo not be ashamed of the ᵇtestimony of our Lord or of me ᶜHis prisoner, but join with *me* in ᵈsuffering for the ᵉgospel according to the power of God,

---

* Because this Observation Worksheet is not printed in color, the references to the author (Paul) and the recipient (Timothy) have been printed in shades of gray. Normally we would use two different colors to distinguish them.

9 who has ᵃsaved us and ᵇcalled us with a holy ᶜcalling, ᵈnot according to our works, but according to His own ᵇpurpose and grace which was granted us in ᵉChrist Jesus from ⁱall eternity,

10 but ᵉnow has been revealed by the ᵇappearing of our Savior ᶜChrist Jesus, who ᵈabolished death and brought life and immortality to light through the gospel,

11 ᶜfor which I was appointed a preacher and an apostle and a teacher.

12 For this reason I also suffer these things, but ᵃI am not ashamed; for I know ᵇwhom I have believed and I am convinced that He is able to ᶜguard what I have entrusted to Him ⁱuntil ᵈthat day.

13 ¹ᵃRetain the ᵇstandard of ᶜsound words ᵈwhich you have heard from me, in the ᵉfaith and love which are in ⁱChrist Jesus.

14 Guard, through the Holy Spirit who ᵃdwells in us, the ¹ᵇtreasure which has been entrusted to you.

Onesiphorus was not ashamed 15 You are aware of the fact that all who are in ¹ᵃAsia ᵇturned away from me, among whom are Phygelus and Hermogenes.

16 The Lord grant mercy to ᵃthe house of Onesiphorus, for he often refreshed me and ᵇwas not ashamed of my ᶜchains;

17 but when he was in Rome, he eagerly searched for me and found me—

18 the Lord grant to him to find mercy from the Lord on ᵃthat day—and you know very well what services he rendered at ᵇEphesus.

How to Use
Word Study Tools

*T*o show you how to use the various word study tools, let's do a word study on a word from 2 Timothy.

In 2 Timothy 1:14, Paul instructs Timothy to "guard, through the Holy Spirit who dwells in us, the treasure which has been entrusted to you." A simple word study of the word "guard," used in this verse, will help us understand this word in this context as Paul and Timothy understood it.

How to Use an Exhaustive Concordance

STEP 1: The first step is to determine which concordance you will be using, because each concordance is keyed to a particular translation. Since some Bibles translate Greek words differently, you need to make sure the concordance you use is based on the same translation as your Bible (i.e. KJV, NASB, NIV, etc.).

We prefer the NASB translation because of its faithfulness to the Greek and because it is a word for word translation. Therefore, we would use the *New American Standard Exhaustive Concordance.*

STEP 2: Look up the word "guard" in the front of the concordance in the section titled "Main Concordance." This concordance works like a dictionary, in that the words are arranged in alphabetical order.

the rear *g* for all the camps,	Nu 10:25	622	who *g* the door of the king's house.	2Ch 12:10	8104
and the rear *g* came after the ark,	Jos 6:9	622	from those who *g* the door,	Es 2:21	8104
and the rear *g* came after the ark	Jos 6:13	622	and I *g* them, and not one of them	Jn 17:12	5442
g on the west side of the city,	Jos 8:13	6119	**GUARDHOUSE**		
and assign men by it to *g* them,	Jos 10:18	8104	Jeremiah to the court of the *g*	Jer 37:21	4307
...ase be on *g* in the morning,	1Sa 19:2	8104	...ained in the court of the *g*.	Jer 37:21	430?
...tain over your *g*,	1Sa ...		...the court of the *g*;	Jer ...	
...o your lor...			...the ...		
praetorian ...	...:13	4232	**GUIDANCE**		
shall *g* your hearts and...	Php 4:7	5432	turning around by His *g*,	Jb 37:12	8458
g what has been entrusted to you,	1Tm 6:20	5442	Where there is no *g*, the people fall,	Pr 11:14	8458
He is able to *g* what I have entrusted	2Tm 1:12	5442	And make war by wise *g*.	Pr 20:18	8458
G. through the Holy Spirit who	2Tm 1:14	5442	For by wise *g* you will wage war,	Pr 24:6	8458
Be on *g* against him yourself, for	2Tm 4:15	5442	**GUIDE**		
beforehand, be on your *g* lest,	2Pe 3:17	5442	by day, To *g* them on their way,	Ne 9:19	5148
children, *g* yourselves from idols.	1Jn 5:21	5442	*g* the Bear with her satellites?	Jb 38:32	5148
GUARDED			sake Thou wilt lead me and *g* me.	Ps 31:3	5095
He *g* him as the pupil of His eye.	Dt 32:10	5431	He will *g* us until death.	Ps 48:14	5090a

1. Looking at the alphabetic guides at the top of the page in the NAS concordance, locate the page that should have the word "guard" on it. In this case, page 505 has the guide words **GROUNDED–GUARD.** The listing for **GUARD,** and all the words between **GROUNDED** and **GUARD** (like **GROW**) will be found on this page. The top of page 506 has the alphabetic guides **GUARDED–GUILT,** because **GUARDED** is the first word that starts on this page. The exact word must lie within the range of the alphabetic guides at the top of the page. You then look down the columns until you find the word "guard." (Notice there are other sections for other forms of "guard," such as "guarded.") Find the book, chapter, and verse for "guard" as used in 2 Timothy 1:14.

These Scripture references are listed in the order of the books of the Bible, then the chapter and verse. In this case, the list of Scriptures that use "guard" begins on page 505 and continues on page 506. As you go down the first column on page 506, you find the listing **2Tm 1:14.**

To the left of the Scripture designation (**2Tm 1:14**) you will find a portion of the verse. The letter 'G' represents the word "guard."

To the right of the Scripture reference you will find a number: *5442.* This is called the reference number and corresponds to the reference number found in _Strong's Exhaustive Concordance_. The Strong's reference number is used in a variety of word study tools. Write down or remember this number, since you will need it later.

2. If you are using _Strong's Exhaustive Concordance_, the process is similar, but you need to look up the King James Version English word which corresponds to "guard" in 2 Timothy 1:14. In the KJV, 2 Timothy 1:14 reads, "That good thing which was committed unto thee <u>keep</u> by the Holy Ghost which dwelleth in us." You see, then, that the word "guard" in the NASB is "keep" in the KJV.

| MAIN CONCORDANCE. | Justice Keep | 559 |

Ge 28: 15 will _k·_ thee in all places whither 8104
      20 and will _k·_ me in this way that I go. "
      30: 31 I will again feed and _k·_ thy flo...
         _k·_ that thou hast unto ...
                                     ...ce. * "
      69 Wi...   ...my whole 5341
      88 I _k·_ the testimony of thy mouth. *8104
      100 because I _k·_ thy precepts.   *5341
      101 way, that I might _k·_ thy word.   *8104
      106 I will _k·_ thy righteous judgments.* "
      115 I will _k·_ the commandments of my 5341
      129 therefore doth my soul _k·_ them.   "
      134 of man: so will I _k·_ thy precepts. *8104
      136 eyes, because they _k·_ not thy law." "
      145 me, O Lord: I will _k·_ thy statutes. 5341
      146 me, and I shall _k·_ thy testimonies.*8104
      127: 1 except the Lord _k·_ the city, the "

Jos 22: 5 to _k·_ his commandments, and to 8104
       23: 6 to _k·_ and to do all that is written i...
          ...will _k·_ the way of the Lord t...
            ...ir fathers did ...
                                     ...4722
2Co 11: 9 u...   ...yself. 5083
Ga 6: 13 who are c...   ...u _k·_ the law; 5442
Eph 4: 3 to _k·_ the unity of the Spirit in the 5083
Ph'p 4: 7 shall _k·_ your hearts and minds *5432
2Th 3: 3 stablish you, and _k·_ you from evil.*5442
1Ti 5: 22 other men's sins: _k·_ thyself pure. 5083
      6: 14 _k·_ this commandment without   "
      20 _k·_ that which is committed to thy *5442
2Ti 1: 12 _k·_ that which I have committed *
      14 unto thee _k·_ by the Holy Ghost * "
Jas 1: 27 to _k·_ himself unspotted from the 5083
      2: 10 whosoever shall _k·_ the whole law, "
1Jo 2: 3 him, if we _k·_ his commandments. "

Look up "keep" in the main concordance. You will notice that in Strong's, the Scripture reference comes before the excerpt of the verse.

These two concordances use the same numbering system, and frequently Strong's uses ditto marks to refer you to the same number used in a Scripture reference above.

STEP 3: The next step is to turn to the Greek dictionary in the back of your concordance and find the reference number of the word you want, in this case _5442_.

All entries in the dictionaries in the back of Strong's and the NAS exhaustive concordances are keyed to the Strong's numbers. There are

151

two dictionaries in the back of your concordance: a Hebrew dictionary and a Greek dictionary. Old Testament words will be found in the Hebrew section; New Testament words in the Greek section. In this instance, be certain that you use the Greek dictionary since you are looking up a New Testament word (the entries in both the Hebrew and Greek dictionaries are numerical, so there are duplicate numbers). Just remember that Old Testament words are in the Hebrew dictionary and New Testament words are in the Greek dictionary.

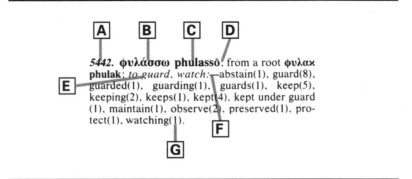

A. The first item you see in the dictionary entry is the Strong's number (**5442**).

B. Then comes the Greek word in the Greek alphabet. If you don't know that alphabet, skip to the next word.

C. The next word is the English transliteration *(phulasso)*. The transliteration is the Greek word spelled with the English alphabet letters that correspond to the sound of the Greek alphabet letters.

D. Then there is a semicolon (;), followed by the etymology or derivation of the word. In this case we learn that *phulasso* comes from a root word, [Greek] *phulak.*

E. Then there is a second semicolon, after which, in italic, comes the definition: *to guard, watch.*

F. After this comes a colon and dash (:—), which precedes a list of all the ways *phulasso* has been translated in the NASB. That is, in various places *phulasso* has been translated as abstain, guard, guarded, guarding, guards, keep, keeping, keeps, kept, kept under guard, maintain, observe, preserved, protect, watching.

G. The numbers in parentheses to the right of each of the words here indicate the number of times that each of these English words appears in the NASB. In other words, *phulasso* has been translated as "abstain" one time (1) somewhere in the NASB, and as "guard" eight times (8), etc.

STEP 4: If you use *Strong's Exhaustive Concordance*, the entries in the Greek dictionary in the back are similar.

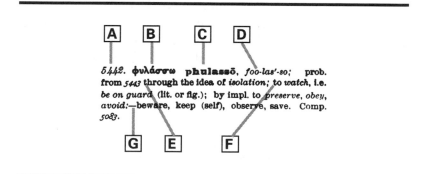

A. First there is the Greek reference number.

B. Then comes the Greek word.

C. Next is the English transliteration.

D. Then there is a phonetic pronunciation of the Greek word. (This is not found in the NAS concordance.)

E. Then comes the derivation of the word.

F. Next is the definition in italic type.

G. Following the colon and dash (:—) are all of the different renderings of the Greek word in the KJV.

H. There is no parenthetical count of the translated words.

153

How to Use an Expository Dictionary

In most cases, as in this one, the dictionary definition from the concordance doesn't provide a great amount of new understanding of the context, but even if it did, the next step is to turn to one or more good expository dictionaries of biblical words, whose chief feature is their definitions.

STEP 1: One of the best known and most widely used is *Vine's Expository Dictionary of New Testament Words*, available in a number of editions from several publishers.

To use Vine's, you will need to have the King James Version English word and the Greek word (transliteration) from your concordance, since that is the order in which entries appear in Vine's.

You know that the KJV English word for the NASB "guard" is "keep," so in Vine's dictionary you look up the word "keep."

Under "keep" you'll find several different Greek words listed. However, you know from your concordance that the Greek transliteration you want is *phulasso,* so look down to the entry with the transliterated form *phulasso.*

There you find:

$\boxed{A}$ $\boxed{B}$ $\boxed{C}$

4. PHULASSŌ (φυλάσσω) denotes (*a*) to guard, watch, keep watch, e.g., Luke 2 : 8 ; in the Passive Voice, 8 : 29 ; (*b*) to keep by way of protection, e.g., Luke 11 : 21 ; John 12 : 25 ; 17 : 12 (2nd part ; No. 1 in 1st part and in ver. 11) ; (*c*) metaphorically, to keep a law, precept, etc., e.g., Matt. 19 : 20 and Luke 18 : 21, " have observed ; " Luke 11 : 28 ; John 12 : 47 (in the best mss.) ; Acts 7 : 53 ; 16 : 4 ; 21 : 24 ; Rom. 2 : 26 ; Gal. 6 : 13 ; 1 Tim. 5 : 21 (" observe ") ; in the Middle Voice, Mark 10 : 20 (" have observed ") ; (*d*) in the Middle Voice, to keep oneself from, Acts 21 : 25 ; elsewhere translated by the verb to beware. See BEWARE, No. 3, GUARD, B, No. 1.

$\boxed{E}$ $\boxed{D}$

A. The transliterated form.

B. The Greek word in the Greek alphabet.

C. The definition—in this case four definitions noted under (a), (b), (c), and (d).

D. Scripture references (although these do not include every instance where the word is used).

E. At the end of the article, Vine indicates that more information might be present under "beware" at entry No. 3, and under "guard," entry No. 1 under B.

Note that 2 Timothy 1:14 is not listed here as one of the Scripture references, so in order to determine the definition, context will have to be your guide.

Here, either definition (a) to guard, watch, keep watch or (b) to keep by way of protection would fit the context, but (c) and (d) don't seem to fit.

STEP 2: A relatively new expository dictionary that will save you time is Zodhiates' *The Complete Word Study Dictionary: New Testament*. The primary advantage of this dictionary is that it is not keyed to a specific English translation of the Bible, so you don't need to find the KJV word when you're studying from the NASB. All entries in this expository dictionary are listed by the same numbers that are used in Strong's and the NAS concordances.

Therefore, to gain more insight into the meaning of "guard," let's look up the Strong's reference number (**5442**) in Zodhiates' dictionary.

Each entry in this dictionary follows the form below, although not all elements are present in each entry:

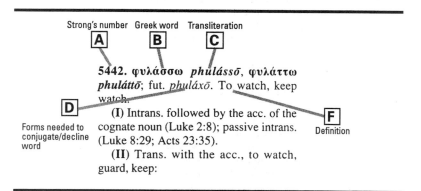

Strong's number Greek word Transliteration
A B C

5442. φυλάσσω *phulássō,* φυλάττω *phulátto;* fut. *phuláxō.* To watch, keep watch.

D
Forms needed to conjugate/decline word

(I) Intrans. followed by the acc. of the cognate noun (Luke 2:8); passive intrans. (Luke 8:29; Acts 23:35).

F
Definition

(II) Trans. with the acc., to watch, guard, keep:

(A) Persons or things from escape or violence (Luke 8:29; Acts 12:4; 28:16). Followed by *en* (1722), in, and the dat. (Acts 23:35); by the acc. (Luke 11:21; Acts 22:20; Sept.: Gen. 2:15; 3:25; 1 Sam. 19:11).

(B) Of persons or things kept in safety, to keep, preserve (John 17:12; 2 Pet. 2:5; Jude 1:24; Sept.: Ex. 23:20; Prov. 6:22). Followed by *apó* (575), from, and the gen. (2 Thess. 3:3; 1 John 5:21, "keep yourselves from idols"); with the acc. (1 Tim. 6:20; 2 Tim. 1:14). With *eis hēméran* (*eis* [1519], unto; *hēméran* [2250], day), unto the day (2 Tim. 1:12); followed by *eis zōén* ([2222], life), "unto life" (John 12:25).

(C) In the mid., to protect oneself, to be on one's guard, to beware of, avoid. In the mid. (Luke 12:15); followed by the acc., to guard against (Acts 21:25; 2 Tim. 4:15). Followed by *hína* (2443) and *mḗ* (3361), not, so that not (2 Pet. 3:17).

G
References

H
Derivatives

Deriv.: *diaphulássō* (1314), to guard thoroughly, protect; *phulakḗ* (5438), the act of guarding; *phulaktḗrion* (5440), phylactery; *phúlax* (5441), a keeper, guard.

I
Synonyms

Syn.: *kratéō* (2902), to hold fast; *sunéchō* (4912), to hold together; *sṓzō* (4982), save, preserve; *blépō* (991), to take heed; *proséchō* (4337), to be on guard, to beware; *horáō* (3708), to behold, pay attention to; *epéchō* (1907), to take heed; *skopéō* (4648), to mark, heed, consider; *phrouréō* (5432), to guard; *tēréō* (5083), to watch over, preserve, keep; *diatēréō* (1301), to keep carefully; *suntēréō* (4933), to preserve, keep safe.

J
Antonyms

Ant.: *lanthánō* (2990), to be unaware; *epilanthánomai* (1950), forget, neglect; *eklanthánomai* (1585), to forget completely; *paradídōmi* (3860), to betray; *eleutheróō* (1659), to make free; *parabaínō* (3845), to transgress; *biázō* (971), to violate; *ameléō* (272), to neglect.

A. Strong's number (same as the NASB concordance number).

B. Greek word.

C. Transliteration.

D. Forms needed to conjugate or decline the word (conjugate = to give in prescribed order the various inflectional forms of words, especially verbs; decline = to give in prescribed order the grammatical forms of a noun, pronoun, or adjective).

E. Identification (gender and part of speech; in this specific entry, neither is mentioned).

F. Definition (sometimes, in addition to the definition, a discussion of the implications of some Greek words for the interpretation of more difficult passages has been given).

G. References.

H. Derivatives.

I. Synonyms (words with similar meaning).

J. Antonyms (words with opposite meaning).

In Zodhiates' dictionary, after the Greek word and transliteration, we see the definition: "to watch, keep watch."

Then, starting with **(I)** we find a variety of usages in various places in Scripture, and under **(II) (B)** we see a reference to 2 Timothy 1:14, which means the definition there applies: "used of persons or things kept in safety, to keep, preserve."

Context always determines the definition of a word, so even when the Scripture is listed, other parts of the article may give additional help in understanding the meaning of a word. When the particular Scripture reference is _not_ listed in the article, context will be the only guide as to which part(s) of the article should be used.

Take What You've Learned Back to the Text

From your work in Strong's and the NAS exhaustive concordances as well as Vine's and Zodhiates' dictionaries you would be able to see that "guard" ("keep" in KJV) in 2 Timothy 1:14 means "to guard, to watch, to keep by way of protection, to keep in safety, to preserve." Now you can take this information back to the text and see that in this context the word "guard" means:

> "Guard [watch, keep in safety, protect, and preserve], through the Holy Spirit who dwells in us, the treasure which has been entrusted to *you.*"

It is at this point that you will begin to appreciate the value of knowing how to do word studies.

However, a word of caution: The text always dictates the meaning of the word. Just choosing a certain definition that sounds good to you or fits with a certain viewpoint and then imposing that meaning into the text is not an accurate handling of God's Word. Context rules in determining the way a word is used.

Review

The procedure for doing a word study is quite straightforward, and as you begin practicing it, you will find that it becomes easier.

1. The front part of the concordance is used to look up the English word (in the Bible translation that matches the concordance translation) to discover the number you need for the Greek or Hebrew dictionary in the back. In the Strong's and NAS concordances these numbers are the same.

2. Then in the back of the concordance go to either the Greek or Hebrew dictionary (depending on whether you are studying a passage from the New or Old Testament) and find the number and the corresponding Greek or Hebrew word.

3. If you are using Zodhiates' dictionary to find the expanded definition, look up the number and read the article.

   Other dictionaries, such as Vine's, are keyed to a specific translation, such as the King James Version. Each dictionary will tell you to which English translation it is keyed.

To find the correct entry in this type of dictionary, you need to know the Greek or Hebrew word as well as the English word.

4. Then take the definition back to the text to see if it helps in your understanding.

Remember that the purpose for doing word studies is to put the definition or meaning of the words back into the text to better understand what it means.

Tense, Voice, and Mood of Verbs

ecause verbs express action, they are often the most signifi-cant elements in the expression of thought and key to under-standing what the author is trying to communicate. Therefore, understanding the Greek verb is a key to correct interpretation and application of Scripture.

Part of the beauty of the Greek language is that the construction of its verbs clearly shows who does the action, whether the statement is a command or a suggestion, and whether the passage is speaking of reality or possibility. In doing this, the major features of Greek verbs are tense, voice, and mood.

By thinking through a simple, concise explanation of tense, voice, and mood, new vistas of insight will be opened to you. Keep in mind that the following is a simplified and nonexhaustive summarization of a complex subject. It is not intended to be a substitute for Greek gram-mars, but will give you an overview of terms that are frequently used in the more technical commentaries. (You will also find this information, along with the easy-to-use charts, in the Appendix of the *New Induc-tive Study Bible*).

TENSE
Shows the Kind of Action

Greek verb tenses differ from English verb tenses in that the kind of action portrayed is the most significant element, and time is a relatively minor consideration.

Action as Continuous

 ∾ **Present tense**: continuous action. This is primarily progressive or linear; it shows action that is continuing.

Examples:

Jeff *is studying* the Bible.

"As the branch *cannot bear* fruit of itself unless it *abides* in the vine, so neither can you unless you *abide* in Me" (John 15:4b).

"If anyone *does not abide* in Me" (John 15:6).

 ∾ **Imperfect tense**: continuous action, usually in the past.

Examples:

Jeff *was studying* the Bible.

"If you were of the world, the world *would love* its own"— literally, "would have been loving" its own (John 15:19a).

Action as Completed

 ∾ **Perfect tense**: punctiliar action in the past with the results continuing into the present. (Punctiliar action is action that happens at a specific point in time.)

Examples:

Jeff is being transformed by *having studied* the Bible.

"You are already clean because of the word which I *have spoken* to you" (John 15:3).

"Just as I *have kept* My Father's commandments and abide in His love" (John 15:10b).

ᑍ **Pluperfect tense**: punctiliar action in the past with the results continuing in the past.

Examples:

Jeff was transformed because he *had studied* the Bible.

"For the Jews *had* already *agreed"* (John 9:22).

Action as Occurring

ᑍ **Aorist tense**: punctiliar action. The aorist tense states that an action occurs without regard to its duration; that is, it denotes the fact of an action without any reference to the length of that action. The aorist tense is like a snapshot that shows (expresses) that an action occurs, while the present tense action is like a moving picture, continuing on.

Examples:

Jeff *studied* the Bible.

"Abide in Me, and I in you" (John 15:4a).

ᑍ **Future tense**: indefinite action to occur in the future. Indicates continuing or punctiliar action in the future.

Examples:

Jeff *will be studying* his Bible.

"It *will be done* for you" (John 15:7).

"So prove to *be* My disciples" (John 15:8).

VOICE
Shows How the Subject
Is Related to the Action

ᑍ **Active voice**: indicates that the subject produces the action.

Examples:

Jeff *hit* the ball.

"And every branch that bears fruit, He *prunes* it" (John 15:2b).

∽ **Passive voice:** indicates that the subject is acted upon.

Examples:

Jeff *was hit* by the ball.

"And they *are burned"* (John 15:6).

∽ **Middle voice:** indicates that the subject initiates the action and also participates in the results of the action. (This voice is unique to Greek construction.)

Examples:

Jeff hit himself with the ball.

"That is the Spirit of truth who *proceeds* from the Father, He will testify about Me" (John 15:26).

One note of interest when looking up a verb in a Greek study tool: The middle and passive voices will have identical forms, but the context will show you if the subject is receiving the action (passive voice) or if the subject initiated the action and participated in it (middle voice).

Also, some verbs are *deponent verbs.* This means that their form in a Greek study tool may be listed as a passive or middle voice verb, but their function or action is active. Usually your Greek study helps will list these as deponent verbs.

MOOD
Shows the Kind of Action

∽ **Indicative mood:** the declarative mood or mood of certainty. This is a statement of fact which assumes reality from the speaker's point of view. This mood simply states a thing as being a fact.

Examples:

Bible study *has changed* Jeff's life.

"He *is thrown* away as a branch and *dries* up; and they *gather* them, and *cast* them into the fire and they *are burned"* (John 15:6).

∾ **Imperative mood:** usually a command or entreaty. It is the mood of volition or will. The imperative mood in the Greek makes a demand on the will of the reader to obey the command; it is used to indicate prohibition and authority.

Examples:

Jeff, *study* your homework.

"Abide in Me" (John 15:4).

"Ask whatever you wish" (John 15:7).

"Abide in My love" (John 15:9).

"Remember the word that I said to you" (John 15:20).

One aspect which will help your study of God's Word is the understanding of the combination of the present tense and the imperative mood that is stating a negative command (a prohibition). The *present imperative prohibition* demands cessation of some act already in progress.

Example:

"Jesus said to her, *'Stop clinging* to Me'" (John 20:17).

In other words, Mary was already clinging to Jesus, and Jesus was telling her to stop clinging and to go on refusing to cling to Him.

∾ **Subjunctive mood:** the mood of probability. This implies some doubt regarding the reality of the action from the speaker's point of view. It expresses an uncertainty or an action which may or should happen. This is the mood used for conditional clauses, strong suggestions, or "polite" commands.

Examples:
Jeff may have done his homework.

(Jeff, if you do not do your homework, you cannot participate in the class discussion.)

"That it *may bear* more fruit" (John 15:2).

165

"As the branch cannot bear fruit of itself unless it *abides* in the vine, so neither can you unless you *abide* in Me" (John 15:4b).

"If anyone *does not abide* in Me" (John 15:6).

"If you *abide* in Me, and My words *abide* in you" (John 15:7).

Something else which may help you in your study of God's Word is an understanding of the combination of the aorist tense and the subjunctive mood that is stating a negative command (a prohibition). The **aorist subjunctive prohibition** is a warning or an exhortation against doing a thing not yet begun.

Example:

Peter said to Him, "*Never shall* You *wash* my feet!" (John 13:8a).

In other words, Peter was telling Jesus that He was not to wash his feet and Jesus was not even to start washing his feet.

~ **Optative mood:** the mood of possibility. This mood presents no definite anticipation of realization but merely presents the action as conceivable from the speaker's point of view. (Used less frequently than the other moods.)

Examples:

I wish my neighbor, Jeff, would take the Precept Bible Studies.

"May the Lord *direct* your hearts" (2 Thessalonians 3:5).

TENSE

The emphasis is on the *kind* of action, not the time of action.

Tense	Kind of Action	Example
Present	Continuous action	Jeff is studying the Bible.
Imperfect	Continuous action in the past	Jeff was studying the Bible.
Perfect	Punctiliar action in the past with the results continuing into the present	Jeff is being transformed by having studied the Bible.
Pluperfect	Punctiliar action in the past with the results continuing in the past	Jeff was transformed because he had studied the Bible.
Aorist	Punctiliar action (The time can be past, present, or future but is generally past.)	Jeff studied the Bible.
Future	Generally continuous action in the future, but on occasion it can be punctiliar.	Jeff will be studying his Bible.

TENSE OF GREEK VERBS

MOOD

The mood expresses the relationship of the action to reality from the speaker's point of view.

Mood	Relation to Reality	Usage or Meaning	Example
Indicative	Mood of certainty (reality)	Used to declare a statement of fact as something which is true. Expresses that which is actual, factual, or real from the speaker's point of view.	Bible study has changed Jeff's life.
Imperative	Mood of volition or will (potential reality)	Usually used to express a command or entreaty. Denotes intention, authority, permission, or prohibition.	Jeff, study your homework.
Subjunctive	Mood of probability (probable reality)	Used to express an action which may or should happen but which is not necessarily true at the present, from the speaker's point of view. Expresses conditional or uncertain actions.	Jeff may have done his homework.
Optative	Mood of possibility (possible reality)	Merely presents an action as conceivable from the speaker's point of view, with no definite anticipation of realization.	I wish my neighbor, Jeff, would take the Precept Bible Studies.

MOOD OF GREEK VERBS

VOICE

The voice expresses the relationship of the subject to the action.

Voice	How the Subject Is Related to the Action	Example
Active	Indicates that the subject produces the action	Jeff hit the ball.
Passive	Indicates that the subject is acted upon	Jeff was hit by the ball.
Middle	Indicates that the subject initiates the action and participates in the results of the action	Jeff hit himself with the ball.

PROHIBITIONS

This is when the speaker states a negative command.

Prohibition	Definition	Example
Present imperative (used with a negative)	This prohibition demands cessation of some act already in progress.	John 20:17
Aorist subjunctive (used with a negative)	This prohibition is a warning or exhortation against doing a thing not yet begun.	John 13:8

VOICE OF GREEK VERBS

How to Discover
Tense, Voice, and Mood

*he purpose of this section is to teach you how to use word study
tools to find the tense, voice, and mood of a Greek verb and then
to use that information to better understand the Scripture.

Complete Word Study New Testament

One reference tool that is easy to use in identifying grammatical constructions, such as verb tense, voice, and mood, is Spiros Zodhiates'
Complete Word Study New Testament. To explain how to use it, let's
continue with our study of the word "guard" in 2 Timothy 1:14.

STEP 1: The first thing you need to do is turn to 2 Timothy 1:14 in the
Complete Word Study New Testament. Since this work uses the KJV
translation, you look for "keep."

---

687   2 TIMOTHY 1:18

pim2192   an,nn5296   pap5198   an,nn3056   repro3739   aina191   pre3844 ppro1700

13 Hold fast the form of sound words, which thou hast heard of me,

pre1722 an,nn4102 2532 an,nn26 art3588   pre1722 an,nn5547 an,nn2424

in faith and love which is in Christ Jesus.

art,aj2570   an,nn3672   aima5442 pre1223   an,aj40

14 That good thing which*was*committed*unto*thee keep by the Holy

an,nn4151   art,pap1774   pre1722 ppro2254

Ghost which dwelleth in us.

depro5124   pin1492   3754 an,aj3956   art3588   pre1722 art,nn773

15 This thou knowest, that all they which are in Asia be

Notice above the word "keep," the code **aima5442**. You recognize, of course, the Strong's reference number (5442), and "aima" is a grammatical code that will be the key to understanding tense, voice, and mood.

Since every word in Zodhiates' *Complete Word Study New Testament* is coded to Strong's, this book can be used in lieu of Strong's to find the number and the Greek word. If you also use Zodhiates' *Word Study Dictionary of New Testament Words*, recall that you use the Strong's number to find the Greek word and its definition.

As you will see later, Zodhiates' *Complete Word Study New Testament* also has the Strong's Greek dictionary and lexical aids to assist in finding word meanings.

Here, however, our purpose is to discover how this tool can show you grammatical information, specifically, tense, voice, and mood.

STEP 2: Returning to the "aima" above the word "keep," let's turn to the next part of Zodhiates' *Complete Word Study New Testament,* the "Grammatical Codes to the Grammatical Notations" chart, which will explain what that code means.

(When you purchase the *Complete Word Study New Testament* you also receive a smaller, laminated chart on a bookmark card to be used as a ready, portable reference that you can move to the passage you are studying.)

GRAMMATICAL CODES TO THE GRAMMATICAL NOTATIONS

The grammatical codes, the small codes in the line above the text of this New Testament, are listed alphabetically below. These codes represent grammatical constructions found in the Greek New Testament. The number(s) in parentheses after each of the codes refer to the particular grammatical notations, found in the Study Helps section, that will explain the construction. For example, the future middle, **fm,** is explained by its own notation **36** (in bold type) with cross references to notations 35 (future tense) and 50 (middle voice).

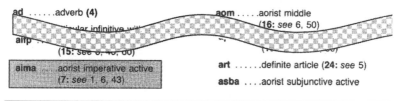

ad . . . . . .adverb **(4)**	aom . . . . .aorist middle
. . . .ular infinitive . . .	**(16:** *see* 6, 50)
aifp . . .	
(15: *see* 6, 46, 66)	
aima . . . .aorist imperative active	art . . . . . .definite article **(24:** *see* 5)
(7: *see* 1, 6, 43)	**asba** . . . .aorist subjunctive active

1. The code chart is listed alphabetically, and the codes represent grammatical constructions found in the Greek New Testament. In this case, you see that the code "aima" means aorist imperative active (**7**: see 1, 6, 43).

2. The number(s) in the parentheses after each of the codes refer to the particular grammatical notation in the "Grammatical Notations" section that will explain the construction. Turn to this section.

   There are 95 grammatical notations, which give definitions of the grammatical categories (such as, what it means that a verb is aorist imperative passive).

GRAMMATICAL NOTATIONS
Definitions of the Grammatical Categories

1. The **Active Voice** represents the action as being accomplished by the subject of the verb: *árti ginóskō ek mérous, tóte de epignósomai, kathós kai epegnósthēn*, "now I know in part; but then shall I know even as also I am known" (1 Cor. 13:12). In Greek it is to be distinguished from the **Middle Voice (50)** and **Passive Voice (60)**. See also **95**.

2. The **Adjective (aj)** is a word which modifies a noun by describing certain properties or qualities of the noun. An adjective can be attributive: *pan déndron agathón karpoús kaloús poieí*, "every good tree bringeth forth good fruit" (Matt. 7:17). It can also be predicative, ⸢...⸣ng an explicit or implied ⸢...⸣ *marturēthē einai dikaios* ⸢...⸣ ⸢...⸣ also are compa⸢...⸣ ⸢...⸣oud of witnesses⸢...⸣ (Heb. ⸢...⸣). See also **24**.

6. The **Aorist Tense** is used for simple, undefined action. In the indicative mood, the aorist tense can indicate punctiliar action (action that happens at a specific point in time) in the past. It must be distinguished from the **Imperfect Tense (44)** which denotes continuous action in the past. With few exceptions, whenever the aorist tense is used in any mood other than the indicative, the verb does not have any temporal significance. In other words, it refers only to the reality of an event or action, not to the time when it took place. See also **95**.

AORIST IMPERATIVE The aorist imperative denotes a command, request, or entreaty. Unlike the **Present Imperative (80, 81)**, it does not involve a command or entreaty for continuous or repetitive action. Instead, it is often used for general exhortations and for things that must be begun at that very moment. See also **6, 43.**

7. The **Aorist Imperative Active (aima):** *nēpsate, grēgorēsate*, "Be sober, be vigilant" ⸢...⸣t 5:8). See also **1.** ⸢...⸣him" (Matt. 27:49).

41. The **Future Participle Middle (fptm):** *ou to sóma to genēsómenon speireis*, "thou sowest not that body that shall be" (1 Cor. 15:37). See also **50.**

42. The **Future Participle Passive (fptp):** *eis martúrion tōn lalēthēsoménōn*, "for a testimony of those things which were to be spoken after" (Heb. 3:5). See also **60.**

43. The **Imperative Mood** is used to give a command: *húpage, seautón deíxon tō hiereí*, "go thy way, show thyself to the priest" (Mark 1:44); an exhortation *poiēsate oun karpoús axíous tēs metanoías*, "Bring forth therefore fruits meet for repentance" (Matt. 3:8); or an entreaty *ton árton hēmōn ton epioúsion dídou hēmīn to kath' hēméran*, "Give us day by day our daily bread" (Luke 11:3). See also **7–9, 20, 62, 80, 81, 95.**

3. Note what aorist imperative means and look at **7: 1, 6, 43** notations:

AORIST IMPERATIVE: The aorist imperative denotes a command, request, or entreaty. Unlike the **Present Imperative (80, 81)**, it does not involve a command or entreaty for continuous or repetitive action. Instead, it is often used for general exhortations and for things that must be begun at that very moment. See also **6, 43.**

7. The **Aorist Imperative Active (aima):** *nepsate, gregoresate,* "Be sober, be vigilant" (1 Pet. 5:8). See also **1.**

4. This entry gives an example from 1 Peter, but no further information, so look at article 1, the Active Voice:

1. The **Active Voice** represents the action as being accomplished by the subject of the verb: *arti ginosko ek merous, tote de epignosomai, kathos kai epegnosthen,* "now I know in part; but then shall I know even as also I am known" (1 Cor. 13:12). In Greek it is to be distinguished from the **Middle Voice (50)** and **Passive Voice (60).** See also **95.**

5. Then look at article 6, the Aorist Tense:

6. The **Aorist Tense** is used for simple, undefined action. In the indicative mood, the aorist tense can indicate punctiliar action (action that happens at a specific point in time) in the past. It must be distinguished from the **Imperfect Tense (44)** which denotes continuous action in the past. **With few exceptions, whenever the aorist tense is used in any mood other than the indicative, the verb does not have any temporal significance.** In other words, it refers only to the reality of an event or action, not to the time when it took place. See also **95.**

6. And finally, look at article 43, the Imperative Mood:

43. The **Imperative Mood** is used to give a command: *hupage, seauton deixon to hierei,* "*go thy way, show* thyself to the priest" (Mark 1:44); an exhortation *poiesate oun karpous axious tes metanoias,* "Bring forth therefore fruits meet for repentance" (Matthew 3:8); or an entreaty *ton arton hemon ton epiousion* *didou* hemin to kath' hemeran, Give us day by day our daily bread" (Luke 11:3). See also **7–9, 20, 62, 80, 81, 95.**

7. Now, take the explanations back to the text.

So the verb "guard" or *phulasso*, which means "to watch, guard, keep in safety, protect or preserve," is used here in the aorist tense which implies that it is punctiliar action. The aorist tense states that an action occurs without regard to its duration; that is, it denotes the fact of an action without any reference to the length of that action. And the aorist tense expresses the action like a snapshot (unlike the present tense action, which is like a moving picture, continuing on).

By the active voice you know that Timothy, the implied subject of the sentence, is to produce the action. He is to do the guarding; it's not done by someone else for him.

You also know that this action is in the imperative mood, which usually implies a command or entreaty. It is the mood of volition or will. The imperative mood makes a demand on the will of the reader to obey the command; it indicates prohibition and authority.

Therefore, the verb "guard" or *phulasso*, as used in 2 Timothy 1:14, means that Timothy is commanded to watch, guard, keep in safety, protect or preserve, the treasure that has been entrusted to him and that he is the one to do that guarding. The verse tells him who his means of guarding is, the Holy Spirit who dwells in him, but Timothy is responsible to produce the action.

A Parsing Guide to the Greek New Testament

Another tool that shows the tense, voice, and mood of Greek verbs is a parsing guide. One of the best known is by Nathan Han, *A Parsing Guide to the Greek New Testament* (published by Herald Press). To use it, however, you also will need a Greek interlinear New Testament so that you can find the Greek word in the actual form found in the parsing guide.

Any Greek interlinear will suffice, such as the *Interlinear Greek-English New Testament* (published by Baker Book House).

Let's continue with our example of "guard" from 2 Timothy 1:14 to see how these word study tools will further enhance our understanding.

STEP 1: Look up 2 Timothy 1:14 in the interlinear New Testament to determine the actual form of the corresponding Greek word for "guard."

The word here is a slightly different form than *phulasso*, which you found in Strong's and Vine's (exhaustive concordances), because the other tools you have used so far give the "root" form of the word. Here in the interlinear you find the word with the proper ending for the grammatical situation in which it is used.

When you use the parsing guide, you will see that the words are listed in the form given in the interlinear. Neither the parsing guide nor the interlinear uses the transliterated forms. It will be the actual Greek word in actual Greek letters.

1:10-18   II TIMOTHY   749

3588	2041	2257	235	2596	2398	4286	2532	5485	3588

τὰ.ἔργα.ἡμῶν, ἀλλὰ   ᵍκατ'ⁱⁱ   ἰδίαν   πρόθεσιν καὶ χάριν τὴν
our works,   but according to his own   purpose   and grace, which

1325	2254	1722	5547	2424	4253	5550†	166

δοθεῖσαν ἡμῖν ἐν χριστῷ Ἰησοῦ πρὸ χρόνων.αἰωνⁱων,
[was] given   us   in   Christ   Jesus   before   the ages of time,

5319	1161	3568	1223	3588	2015†	3588	4990	2257

10 φανερωθεῖσαν.δὲ νῦν διὰ τῆς ἐπιφανείας τοῦ.σωτῆρος.ἡμῶν
but made manifest   now by   the   appearing   of our Saviour

2424	5547	2673	3303	3588	2288	5461

ʰἸησοῦ χριστοῦ,ᵏ καταργήσαντος μὲν τὸν θάνατον, φωτίσαν-
Jesus   Christ,   who annulled   death,   ʰbrought ³to

1161	2222†	2532	861	1223	3588	2098	1519	3739

τος δὲ ζωὴν καὶ ἀφθαρσίαν διὰ τοῦ εὐαγγελίου, 11 εἰς ὃ
⁴light ¹and life   and incorruptibility by   ᵗʰᵒ glad tidings;   to which

5087	1473	2783	2532	652	2532	1320

ἐτέθην ἐγὼ κήρυξ καὶ ἀπόστολος καὶ διδάσκαλος
²was ³appointed ¹I   a herald and   apostle   and   teacher

1484†	1223	3739	156†	2532	5023	3958	235	3756

ⁱἐθνῶν·ⁱⁱ 12 δι'.ἣν αἰτίαν καὶ ταῦτα πάσχω· ἀλλ' οὐκ
of [the] nations.   For which cause also these things I suffer; but   ³not

1870	1492	1063	3739	4100	2532	3982	3754

ἐπαισχύνομαι, οἶδα.γὰρ ᾧ πεπίστευκα, καὶ πέπεισμαι ὅτι
¹I ²am ashamed;   for I know whom I have believed, and am persuaded that

1415	2076	3588	3866	3450	5442	1519	1565

δυνατός ἐστιν τὴν παραθήκην   μου φυλάξαι εἰς ἐκείνην
able   he is the deposit committed [to him] of me to keep for   that

3588	2250	5296	2192	5198	3056	3739

τὴν ἡμέραν. 13 ὑποτύπωσιν ἔχε ὑγιαινόντων λόγων, ὧν
day.   ²A ³delineation ¹have   of sound   words, which [words]

3844	1700	191	1722	4102	2532	26	3588	1722	5547

παρ' ἐμοῦ ἤκουσας, ἐν πίστει καὶ ἀγάπῃ τῇ   ἐν χριστῷ
from   me thou didst hear, in   faith and   love   which [are] in   Christ

2424	3588	2570†	3872	5442	1223

Ἰησοῦ. 14 τὴν καλὴν ʲπαρακαταθήκηνⁱⁱ φύλαξον διὰ
Jesus.   The good   deposit committed [to thee]   keep   by [the]

4151†	40†	3588	1774	1722	2254	1492	5124

πνεύματος ἁγίου τοῦ ἐνοικοῦντος ἐν ἡμῖν. 15 Οἶδας τοῦτο,
²Spirit ¹Holy which   dwells   in   us.   Thou knowest this,

3754	654	3165	3956	3588	1722	3588	773	3739	2076

ὅτι ἀπεστράφησάν με πάντες οἱ   ἐν τῇ Ἀσίᾳ, ὧν ἐστιν
that turned away from me   all   who [are] in   Asia, of whom is

Left marginal column text:

to our works, but according to his own purpose and grace, which was given us in Christ Jesus before the world began, 10 but is now made manifest by the appearing of our Saviour Jesus Christ, who hath abolished death, and hath brought life and immortality to light through the gospel: 11 whereunto I am appointed a preacher, and an apostle, and a teacher of the Gentiles. 12 For the which cause I also suffer these things: nevertheless I am not ashamed: for I know whom I have believed, and am persuaded that he is able to keep that which I have committed unto him against that day. 13 Hold fast the form of sound words, which thou hast heard of me, in faith and love which is in Christ Jesus. 14 That good thing which was committed unto thee keep by the Holy Ghost which dwelleth in us. 15 This thou knowest, that all they which are in Asia be turned away from me; of whom are Phygellus and Hermogenes. 16 The Lord give mercy unto the house of Onesiphorus; for he oft refreshed me, and was not ashamed of my chain: 17 but, when he was in Rome, he sought me out very diligently, and found me. 18 The Lord grant unto him that he may find mercy of the Lord in that day: and in

STEP 2: Once you have the Greek word from the interlinear, turn to the table of contents in Han's parsing guide. Here you'll find the books of the New Testament written in Greek. (You may want to take the time to write the English equivalent on the Contents page.) Look up the book that you want. In this case you will first find the Greek words for "2 Timothy" in the interlinear and then find them on the Contents page.

CONTENTS

From this, you see that you need to turn to page 387 for 2 Timothy.

Προς Τιμοθεον β΄
1

πέπεισμαι 1 p. sing. perf. pass. ind. . . . . .πείθω
φυλάξαι 1 aor. act. infin. . . . . .φυλάσσω
13 ἔχε 2 p. sing. pres. act. imper. . . . . .ἔχω
ὑγιαινόντων pres. act. ptc. gen. pl. masc. . . . . ὑγιαίνω
ἤκουσας 2 p. sing. 1 aor. act. ind. . . . . ἀκούω
14 φύλαξον 2 p. sing. 1 aor. act. imper. . . . . . . φυλάσσω
ἐνοικοῦντος pres. act. ptc. gen. sing. neut. . . . ἐνοικέω
15 οἶδας 2 p. sing. perf. act. ind. . . . . οἶδα
ἀπεστράφησαν 3 p. pl. 2 aor. pass. ind. . . . . ἀποστρέφω
16 δώη 3 p. sing. 2 aor. act. opt. . . . . .δίδωμι
ἀνέψυξεν 3 p. sing. 1 aor. act. ind. . . . . . . .ἀναψύχω
ἐπαισχύνθη 3 p. sing. 1 aor. pass. ind. . . .ἐπαισχύνομαι
17 γενόμενος 2 aor. mid. ptc. nom. sing. masc. . . .γίνομαι
ἐζήτησεν 3 p. sing. 1 aor. act. ind. . . . . ζητέω
εὗρεν 3 p. sing. 2 aor. act. ind. . . . . εὑρίσκω
18 εὑρεῖν 2 aor. act. infin. . . . . id.
διηκόνησεν 3 p. sing. 1 aor. act. ind. . . . . . .διακονέω
γινώσκεις 2 p. sing. pres. act. ind. . . . . γινώσκω

The title on the top of the page is 2 Timothy, written in Greek, and listed on the page—in verse order—are all the verbs in 2 Timothy in the form in which they are found in the Greek text.

Since you are investigating "guard" from 2 Timothy 1:14, go down to verse 14. Here you find two Greek verbs listed. From your work in the interlinear you should be able to find *phuladzon*, the form of *phulasso* used here (at the right margin you see *phulasso*, the transliteration given in Strong's, etc.).

You will also see that the entry tells us that this form is **2 p. sing. 1 aor. act. imper.**

> **2 p. sing.** = second person singular
>
> the form of the verb needed to accompany "you."
>
> **1 aor. act. imper.** = first aorist, active, imperative
>
> the tense, voice, and mood of the verb.

You don't need to be concerned with what "first" aorist means, only that the verb is aorist.

Since your interest is in the tense, voice, and mood of the verb, at this point refer back to the section that describes the implication of aorist, active, imperative.

Recommended Study Helps

෬෨෬෬

Books on Inductive Bible Study

Jenson, Irving L. *Independent Bible Study.* Revised. Chicago, Illinois: Moody Press, 1992.

McQuilkin, J. Robertson. *Understanding and Applying the Bible.* Revised Edition. Chicago, Illinois: Moody Press, 1992.

Bible Concordances

Goodrick, Edward and Kohlenberger III, John R. *The NIV Exhaustive Concordance.* Grand Rapids, Michigan: Zondervan, 1990.

Strong, James. *Strong's Exhaustive Concordance of the Bible.* McLean, Virginia: MacDonald Publishing Company.

Thomas, Robert, ed. *New American Standard Exhaustive Concordance of the Bible.* Nashville, Tennessee: A.J. Holman, 1981.

Hebrew and Greek Dictionaries

Richards, Lawrence. *Expository Dictionary of Bible Words.* Grand Rapids, Michigan: Zondervan, 1985.

Vine, W.E., Unger, M.F., and White, W. Jr., eds. *Vine's Complete Expository Dictionary of Old and New Testament Words.* Nashville, Tennessee: Thomas A. Nelson, 1985.

Zodhiates, Spiros. *The Complete Word Study Dictionary: Old Testament*. Chattanooga, Tennessee: AMG Publishers, 1993.

Zodhiates, Spiros. *The Complete Word Study Old Testament*. Chattanooga, Tennessee: AMG Publishers, 1993.

Zodhiates, Spiros. *The Complete Word Study Dictionary: New Testament*. Chattanooga, Tennessee: AMG Publishers, 1992.

Zodhiates, Spiros. *The Complete Word Study New Testament*. Chattanooga, Tennessee: AMG Publishers, 1991.

Word Study Helps

Robertson, Archibald Thomas. *Word Pictures in the New Testament*. Nashville, Tennessee: Broadman Press, 1981.

Wuest, Kenneth S. *Wuest's Word Studies from the New Testament*. Grand Rapids, Michigan: Kregel Publications, 1978.

General Reference Works

Baxter, J. Sidlow. *Explore the Book*. Grand Rapids, Michigan: Zondervan, 1973.

Gower, Ralph and Wight, Fred H. *The New Manners and Customs of Bible Times*. Chicago, Illinois: Moody Press, 1987.

Greek Study Books

Han, Nathan E. *A Parsing Guide to the Greek New Testament*. Scottdale, Pennsylvania: Herald Press, 1971.

Marshall, Alfred. *The Interlinear Greek-English New Testament*. Grand Rapids, Michigan: Zondervan, 1979.

HARVEST HOUSE BOOKS
BY KAY ARTHUR

∾∾∾∾

God, Are You There?
God, Help Me Experience More of You
God, How Can I Live?
God, I Need More Comfort
How to Study Your Bible
Israel, My Beloved
Jesus, God's Gift of Hope
Just a Moment with You, God
Lord, Teach Me to Pray in 28 Days
A Marriage Without Regrets
A Marriage Without Regrets Study Guide
Prayers to Bless Your Marriage
Speak to My Heart, God
With an Everlasting Love

Bibles
The New Inductive Study Bible (NASB)

Discover 4 Yourself®
Inductive Bible Studies for Kids
How to Study Your Bible for Kids
Lord, Teach Me to Pray for Kids
God's Amazing Creation (Genesis 1–2)
Digging Up the Past (Genesis 3–11)
Abraham—God's Brave Explorer (Genesis 11–25)
Joseph—God's Superhero (Genesis 37–50)
Wrong Way, Jonah! (Jonah)
Jesus in the Spotlight (John 1–11)
Jesus—Awesome Power, Awesome Love (John 11–16)
Jesus—To Eternity and Beyond! (John 17–21)
Boy, Have I Got Problems! (James)
God, What's Your Name?

BOOKS IN THE NEW INDUCTIVE STUDY SERIES

༄ ༄ ༄ ༄

Teach Me Your Ways
Genesis, Exodus,
Leviticus, Numbers,
Deuteronomy

*Choosing Victory,
Overcoming Defeat*
Joshua, Judges, Ruth

Desiring God's Own Heart
1 & 2 Samuel,
1 Chronicles

Walking Faithfully with God
1 & 2 Kings, 2 Chronicles

*Overcoming Fear
and Discouragement*
Ezra, Nehemiah, Esther

*Trusting God
in Times of Adversity*
Job

*God's Blueprint for
Bible Prophecy*
Daniel

*Opening the Windows
of Blessings*
Haggai, Zechariah,
Malachi

The Call to Follow Jesus
Luke

*The Holy Spirit
Unleashed in You*
Acts

*Experiencing the Real
Power of Faith*
Romans

*God's Answers for
Relationships and Passions*
1 & 2 Corinthians

*Free from Bondage
God's Way*
Galatians, Ephesians

That I May Know Him
Philippians, Colossians

*Standing Firm in
These Last Days*
1 & 2 Thessalonians

*Walking in Power,
Love, and Discipline*
1 & 2 Timothy, Titus

*Living with Discernment
in the End Times*
1 & 2 Peter, Jude

Behold, Jesus Is Coming!
Revelation